THE
BOOKKEEPING
PRACTICE BLUEPRINT

A Step-by-Step Guide to Building a Thriving Practice with Delighted Clients and the Income & Lifestyle You Want and Deserve

JEANNIE SAVAGE

The Bookkeeping Practice BluePrint
Jeannie Savage

First published in Australia by Jeannie Savage 2025
www.thestrategicbookkeeper.global

A catalogue record for this
book is available from the
National Library of Australia

ISBN: 978-0-6456951-2-0 (pbk)
ISBN: 978-0-6456951-3-7 (ebk)

Typesetting and design by Publicious Book Publishing
Published in collaboration with Publicious Book Publishing
www.publicious.com.au

Contents

This book is dedicated to my Tribe - The members of my Transformation Program.

The space we've created to work together to positively impact one another, personally and professionally, overflows my cup.

Thank you for your trust, your grit, your determination, your courage and your love.

Every day of this journey with you is incredible.

Thank you.

Chapter 1 - Welcome to The Bookkeeping Practice BluePrint.

Hi, I'm Jeannie, and right now I'm excited. Why? Because I am about to share with you my Bookkeeping Practice BluePrint – your step-by-step guide to success, and the planning, diagnostic and day-to-day tool that will help maximise and sustain that success.

In this book, we'll cover a range of topics that will give you clear instructions on how to use the BluePrint I've developed over 13 long years. We'll start with a crash course in Getting it Done, which will help you develop the mindset, the habits and the processes that you'll need. And then we'll move onto the mechanics of getting it done using the BluePrint – your Foundations, Products and Pricing, Finding and Engaging Your Audience, and putting on your Business Development Hat. And believe me, by the time we get to that last chapter, your new Business Development Hat will not only fit and look fabulous on you, but you will also feel incredibly comfortable wearing it.

We have a lot to cover in a few short chapters, but there's some housekeeping to deal with before we dig in. I need to properly introduce myself and explain my credentials so you know why you can trust my knowledge, my experience and my empathy with what you're trying to achieve – because I've been through it all myself.

But the first thing to talk about is taking a step back.

Have you tasted My Secret Sauce?

Have you read my first book? It's called *The Strategic Bookkeeper - My secret sauce recipe for how to build a thriving practice by becoming a strategic bookkeeper.* If you have already read it (and you probably go back to it quite a lot) you can pop through to the next subheading and learn a little more about me. But if you haven't read *The Strategic Bookkeeper*, you can grab a complimentary copy of the e-book at https://www.thestrategicbookkeeper.global/blueprintresources and I strongly recommend that you do so.

There are a lot of concepts, ideas and practices detailed in the first book that we'll be talking about here, so it's really important that you read it and take all that crucial information on board so that using the BluePrint comes easily and quickly to you.

The Strategic Bookkeeper is available at pretty much every online bookstore globally in all forms, and if you haven't read it yet, you need to put this book down and grab it. Play the Long Game and go step-by-step, because that's how we'll get it done together.

You may be tempted to read on before reading my first book and you can but I'm not going to repeat all the concepts it contains here. I want to give you a second phase so to speak, to build on the first book with new thought leadership and a new way to look at how to build and maintain a profitable practice that brings you Joy.

Audio is easy.

Everything I create, I create for busy multitasking parents like me, and most probably like you too. And the simple, entertaining and effective way to absorb the wisdom and practicalities of *The Strategic Bookkeeper* is to grab the audiobook. "I have so much free time to read books and swan about," said no one ever these days – so using your multitasking time like driving, doing housework, working out at the gym, walking and so on to educate yourself, is ok. That's how you'll get it done.

It's really easy to listen to, and you can get it on almost any book or audio platform, including Amazon, Spotify Premium, Audible (which also works with Kindle), Google Play, Apple Books and more, and it's available on my website.

The audiobook is less than six hours long, and it's really easy and informative to listen to while you go about your daily tasks, so why don't you and I agree on a bit of a challenge? Grab that book now and commit to listening to me read it to you over the next seven days, one hour a day. Why? Because that book will change your business and in turn your life.

As will this book.

Ok, would you like to know a little bit about me?

I know you're keen to get into the substance of the BluePrint, and I promise we will very shortly. But first let's get to know each other. When you read my first book, you'll find out a fair bit about me. You'll learn that I'm a mum (maybe like you), that I'm a business and bookkeeping practice veteran and that I've made it my mission to share my success with people like you, so you can experience it too.

You can read all that and much more in *The Strategic Bookkeeper.*

But there are some other things that will be useful to know about me, beyond what I've already shared in my first book. And it's just a few words, so stay with me.

My 'Why'.

You may ask, *Jeannie, why do you invest so much time and energy into sharing the secrets of the Strategic Bookkeeper, and now your BluePrint?* And it's a great question.

For years while running my own bookkeeping practice, in the pit of my stomach, I've had this burning desire to help women all over the world to do better and to be better. I don't just *want* to help women achieve the kind of freedom I have, I need to. Because no woman, no person should be bound by their job, their partner, their circumstances, to do something they don't want to do.

I know from my own experience that the key to that kind of freedom is financial independence. That's a lesson I learned the hard way – I needed financial independence for myself so that I had "choice".

The choice to stay in or leave my marriage. The choice to take care of myself and my children. The choice to make my own decisions and take responsibility for my own success and happiness.

When I finally got there, having the *income* and the *time*, meant I was able to prioritise my physical, mental and spiritual health. I learnt to start putting myself and my family first and now, that's what I want for all women.

Do I serve men too? Hell yes. But I'm also a woman who passionately loves supporting women.

In terms of my ability to help you...

The short answer is, I've been there done that!

Yup, I have seen it all. From a start as humble as you can imagine, through all kinds of problems – growing pains, client and staff difficulties, cashflow constraints, frustrations, tears and sheer determination – I've achieved the kind of success we all want – a 6-figure income plus, lots of time wealth. And because I think every woman deserves the chance to enjoy the kind of success I now take so much pride in, I've bundled my experiences all up into a world class system that anyone can understand and put to work.

I have become the global leader in Branding, Marketing and Selling for Bookkeepers, which is recognised with multiple awards.

Developing my BluePrint.

How long did it take me to dial into my practice, everything in this BluePrint? 13 years! Yes, I achieved a lifestyle practice within five years of starting my journey, but five years in my business wasn't unshakable and unbreakable. The truth is, at that time I didn't fully understand why I was enjoying the success I was – how I'd got to that point. And while it's a bitter pill to swallow, if you don't understand your own recipe for success your business is very much breakable.

After a much-needed sabbatical enjoying the fruits of my success (income and time), I spent the time and money to forensically dissect my success. Yes, I wanted to take my good business and make it great. But more than that, I knew that I'd created something powerful, something that anyone with an ounce of intelligence and a pound of perseverance could replicate, and I wanted to package up everything I learned and built to support others all around the world.

And here we are, with my second book – *The Bookkeeping Practice BluePrint.*

This book is your BluePrint Guide.

Like my first book, The Bookkeeping Practice BluePrint is a how-to guide. And like my first book, the way to approach it is to read it once through for a general understanding, then go through it chapter by chapter and page by page to implement all the ideas and strategies I'll give you.

Please, please, please read The Strategic Bookkeeper first.

I know I said this before, but it bears repeating – you'll get so much more out of this book if you read *The Strategic Bookkeeper* first. You'll 'get' all my references to the essential elements of a successful strategic bookkeeping practice, from creating your brand and developing your menu, to attracting and converting clients and then expanding your relationship with them, to how to shape your systems and your team, and much more.

So what is the BluePrint?

The BluePrint is a visual matrix. A mind map that gives you a ready reference that will help you build your business the same way I built mine, only with your own stamp on it. On one side, the BluePrint tells you everything you need to have in place before you even talk to a client, and on the other side it shows you how to create a pipeline that gives you step-by-step instructions on finding, engaging, nurturing and developing your clients to get the spectacular results you want.

It's a tool you'll use every single day, and in time it will become second nature to you – you won't have to think too hard about how to generate and sustain success, because you'll have all the systems, procedures and most importantly the mindsets in place.

We all need a BluePrint.

If you're like I was early on in my journey, you probably feel alone in the wilderness and need direction. Or maybe, like many bookkeepers I work with, you're busy (or getting busy) but you've realised that you're "building busy", not building "thriving". That's why you, like me, need a BluePrint.

How I created The BluePrint.

Not long after launching The Transformation Program, while learning from my tribe, I decided it would be helpful to create mind maps and flowcharts to deepen learning and help members implement my ideas. That was when the first iteration of the BluePrint was born.

I didn't know then how central it would become. How all roads would lead back to it. How it would become a diagnostics tool and a checklist. That I'd use it weekly in every live coaching session.

I love my BluePrint – and *we* love this BluePrint. I hope you love it and use it and learn from it too. Here's how to do that.

How to use the BluePrint.

Use this link: <u>https://www.thestrategicbookkeeper.</u> <u>global/blueprintresources</u> to find the BluePrint.

I'm going to ask you to use the BluePrint in very much the same way that my tribe and I use it inside my program.

The first thing to do is print it – in colour. In fact, print several copies. Keep it where you can see it. I have a copy on my desk at all times, plus, usually a copy on my kitchen table. You might want to stick it to your bathroom mirror and on the back of your toilet door.

This is the BluePrint that has the power to change your business and your life too, so yeah, you're going to want to look at it. A lot. Some days multiple times.

In the following chapters I will explain what it all means. It's okay if you look at the BluePrint but at first you don't understand all of what's on there. But make no mistake, when you do understand it, it will help you build an unbreakable unshakable bookkeeping practice that gives you the rewards of time and money, and raving fan clients. The dream you imagined from the beginning is all available, you just have to learn how to build and implement it all – and the BluePrint is your master plan to do just that.

Using the BluePrint as a Diagnostics Tool.

Something I really love about the BluePrint is that first and foremost it's a diagnostic tool – you can look at each element and assess whether you've got it dialed in, or whether it's an area you need to work on.

Let me give you an example. As I write this, I'm looking at the BluePrint – specifically, the product ladder. If you've read my first book, you'll know what a product ladder is, and I'll touch on it again in later chapters. Even if you don't know what a product ladder is, if you're a self-employed bookkeeper you have got a product ladder or the bones of one because your core bookkeeping service is right there on your product ladder.

And so even if right now you don't really understand what a product ladder is, you can say to yourself, okay well I've got core products so I'll tick that off.

But the exciting and interesting thing about core products is that when you have the rest of the product ladder in place, you'll sell more of those core products at much higher prices.

So if you were looking at the BluePrint right now, and using it as a diagnostic tool, you might be saying to yourself, "well product ladder is definitely an area I need to work on."

It's important, though, that you don't let that sort of thing get you down. If you use the BluePrint as a diagnostics tool and think to yourself, "I don't have much of this dialed in at all," don't despair. Later on, I'll introduce you to mindset, productivity and mechanics that will help you get it done. For now, just take a moment to embrace the idea that if we work together and you play the Long Game, your success is inevitable. Set your expectation right now... I can do this and together we will do this, okay?

Using the BluePrint as a To-Do List.

Once you've used the BluePrint as a diagnostics tool to look at what you think you already have in place versus what you need to learn and build and implement, you can use it as a to-do list. You can go step by step building and implementing it all, using both my books to help you.

A word on my starter membership.

Using this book along with my first book – and complemented by my podcast – I think you'll be motivated to join my transformation program. But if for some reason you aren't ready to become a full member of my tribe, I recommend my starter membership. Named "starter" because it's a great place to start. In fact, many of our successful tribe members inside my program started there too. You can find a link to my starter membership here: https://www. thestrategicbookkeeper.global/starter

I love my starter membership for too many reasons to mention here. What I really want you to know right now about it is that if you are not inside my transformation program, joining me in the starter membership is the second best way that we can work together.

With a starter membership, which is crazy affordable, you get access to a Vault of tools and resources, plus a monthly mastermind with me. I'll keep you updated and I'll connect with you in a way that's simply impossible on social media or via email.

Building and maintaining a highly profitable and enjoyable bookkeeping practice is a lot like putting a jigsaw together – until you put all the pieces of the puzzle in place you won't get the picture on the box. I like to call that picture "my dream on my terms", or rather your dream on your terms – the income, the lifestyle and the priorities you want. And with a Starter Membership, I'll help you figure out what your picture looks like.

Introducing my tribe.

One of the things I'll be doing throughout this book is sharing the experiences of various members of my 'tribe' with you. That is, the members of my program, who have benefited from becoming part of my Transformation Program.

We give them a money back guarantee on results. Do they have to work for it? Yes. Are they knocking it out of the ballpark? Absolutely. Which means, my system works over and over again. In this book I'll share stories from the tribe to illustrate how they're working the Program and the BluePrint to get results.

An immediate benefit.

If you're considering joining my Transformation Program, there's a time saving in it for you already. You'll only have to read (or better yet, listen to) both my books right through <u>once*</u>, and then you'll have a base level of knowledge that will turbo charge your results inside the program. Because as a member of my tribe, pretty much everything I describe in both my books is done for you and with you.

As we progress through this book, I'll let you know what's done-for-you (and with you) in my program, so you don't need to hire people and build things that we'll give you if you join. So that's a huge cost saving too.

To find out more about the Transformation Program you can visit this page: https://www.thestrategicbookkeeper.global/tsb

And tune into these 3 podcasts - episode 86, 87 and 88 https://www.thestrategicbookkeeper.global/the-strategic-bookkeeper-podcast

And if you have more questions about the program that aren't answered online, or you'd simply like to speak to a human, you can book a call here or, drop us an email hello@thestrategicbookkeeper.global

And yes, a Starter Membership includes a digital and audio copy of The Strategic Bookkeeper. So there's another saving as well.

*If you don't join, take my advice – read each book through once, then *work* through each book carefully a second time.

Accept the Challenge!

I would absolutely love it if you'd jump into my link https://www.facebook.com/groups/thestrategicbookkeepersway and create a post that says, "Challenge accepted". If you do that, I'll comment on it personally. I love my Facebook community and I check Facebook at all hours of the day and night to keep in touch. Because as you will discover as you read my books and engage with me, The Strategic Bookkeeper Project is my life's work and I believe one of my greatest purposes in life.

That's Chapter One done and dusted.

From here on in it's pretty full on, so buckle up – you're about to learn how to turn your practice into a massive ongoing success that will give you not just the income but the time-wealth to enjoy your dream on your terms.

Chapter 2 - Getting it Done.

You've already seen the BluePrint, but at this stage it probably doesn't mean much to you because like anything, you need to learn how to work it. You need to understand every one of the terms and concepts I've used to create the BluePrint, and you need to have the skills, the motivation and the tools to implement them all.

But before you can do that, you need to train yourself in the three-step linear process that is essential to successfully implementing the BluePrint. Incidentally, you can see now why I recommend that you read both my books twice – once for a sense of what they're all about, and the second time to really learn and internalise what I'm saying. This three-step process is a perfect example of something that's super easy to understand on the surface, but takes deeper understanding and work to really internalise.

If you join my Transformation Program you'll be working through each of these steps with us, and believe me, that makes it much easier. But of course, it's up to you.

The 3 Steps.

In my experience, working with bookkeepers inside my program and outside it, the three-step linear process you'll need to master to effectively implement the BluePrint is:

1. Mindset
2. Productivity
3. Mechanics

In short, mindset is about how we think and feel and it influences everything. I mean absolutely everything. Productivity is like time architecture – it's 100% necessary for building your dream business and life. And mechanics refers to all the things you need to learn and build and do. And to tell you the truth, most people think that it's all about mechanics so they jump to that part while neglecting the crucial steps of mastering mindset and productivity.

Just discovering that – learning it from the entrepreneurs and bookkeepers I have worked with – has been mind-blowing for me. Because, and let me be Crystal Clear my friend – mechanics cannot and will not work unless you get your mindset and productivity right.

Inside my signature program we are always working on these three personal resources you'll need to cultivate. So let's dive deeper into each one of these important assets you'll need to develop to successfully put the BluePrint to work for you.

Step 1: Mindset.

I think mindset is the first big domino that many bookkeepers don't get past. Specifically, I'd like to deal with the negative beliefs and emotions that can hold us back from achieving our potential – mindsets that can be a drag.

And while we can all experience a lot of unwelcome mental health / mindset symptoms (anxiety and so on), there are five major root causes that, in my experience act like dominoes in sequence:

1. Shame and self-sabotage.
2. Comparison (the thief of joy).
3. Fail mindset (playing the short game).
4. Fear, doubt, indecision
5. Insecurity

Now I could easily write an entire book on mindset because it's something I work on every day and which plays such a huge role in my success. But for now I'm just going to give you the headlines, and set you on the path to valuing and working on your own strong healthy mindset.

Shame and self-sabotage.
Shame is that voice that taps you on your shoulder and says *who do you think you are? You're not good enough. Hah, I told you you'd fail*!

I base my understanding and approach to dealing with shame and self-sabotage on Brené Brown's work on shame and vulnerability, and I highly recommend her to you. She will open your mind to so much.

In Brené's research, and certainly in my experience, learning to accept shame – which is the human condition – is one hundred percent the key to mental health and happiness.

Shame is the domino that makes the other dominoes fall when it comes to mindset. It's the one that leads to all the other major barriers to success. I know you've felt it too – trying to hold shame at bay creates a swirling subconscious mess. It leads to comparing yourself to others and coming off second best, and that leaves you feeling like a failure. From there it's so easy to get locked in a place of fear, doubt and indecision and suddenly you find yourself trapped in insecurity.

First up, don't think you're unique in experiencing shame. We all suffer from it at some stage, because as I say, it's the human condition. It's all about how we deal with it.

When shame taps me on the shoulder, I say Hi! I lean in, and I invite shame in, to come out from the shadows and sit across from me. My shame looks like a big green blob and it always looks embarrassed – because that's shame isn't it? It tries to keep us embarrassed, and it tells us we're silly and we're not good enough.

The thing is, when you try and keep it at bay, it can simply ooze out the sides as self-sabotage and worse. As we learn from Brene Brown, the key is to fully accept shame which requires vulnerability.

Based on my own experience, I recommend you try doing what I do - when you see shame (and let me tell you, shame is really good at hiding in the shadows), recognise and invite shame in. I hope you find, like me, that this frees you from the effects of shame.

In my own experience, I find shame wears many different dresses and so it can be tricky to recognise him - but when I do I'm like "bingo", there you are! Ahhh, I see you shame, I didn't know that was you, come in you bugger! Let's rumble.

When I invite shame in, he has nothing to say... he's harmless.

Now, I've really only scratched the surface here in order to help you with what I believe is the domino from which other mental health dominoes fall. For more reading on shame and vulnerability, and rising above these and other mindsets that can hold you back, do check out Brené Brown's books, podcasts, videos and more. I love all her work but as a leader (and you are a leader in your business), I particularly love her book *Dare to Lead.*

Success Mindset
So, to reiterate, generating a success mindset is, for a lot of us, about overcoming the barrier emotions and feelings that would hold us back. It's about...

1. Accepting shame as the human condition, and always doing the work to sit with shame and hold space for it. You might even make shame your ally!
2. Not comparing yourself to others, because it is non-productive and will be a drag on your mindset.
3. Taking a patient, long game approach to building the business and life of your dreams. And knowing in your heart that with the right help your success is inevitable.
4. Replacing the idea of "failing" with "refining" – Edison made over a thousand attempts at inventing the light bulb, but he never quit. He had a no-fail mindset because he replaced the idea of "I failed" with "I'm not quite there yet".

Lastly, beware of the paralysing combination of fear, doubt and indecision – when we freeze rather than act. It's a domino that falls in order after the other dominoes, and ironically it makes us feel like we're safe, because if we freeze nothing can go wrong right? Fear, doubt and indecision will rob you of opportunities and your dreams. Do the work, let go of fear, doubt and indecision.

A gift from me.
Two of my favourite gifts are food and knowledge, and this one combines both. If you want to permanently improve your mindset and all other parts of your health, read *Deep Nutrition* by Dr Cate Shanahan (I recommend the audiobook). It changed my life.

This is just the beginning.
There's so much more I want to say on mindset because I know how important it is, and I hope that one day we will work together more on this subject.

If you join my Transformation Program let me be crystal-clear that your success is inevitable. When you embrace exactly what I can teach you around mindset, you become productive and you follow the step-by-step mechanics I provide. My program is a world-class, world-first bookkeeping practice in a box that my members describe as mind blowing. I'm not going to be shy about telling you that. I'm so proud of the contribution I'm making to our industry and the beautiful humans I serve.

Step 2: Productivity (time architecture).

Over the years I have become a productivity ninja - maybe because I value time so much and because unless you manage time, time will manage you. The one thing productivity has in common with mindset is that I could probably write a book on productivity too (stay tuned for that one). But for now, I'm going to keep this short and sweet, but also point you in the direction of some great resources.

Let's start by looking at what I do in my business and my life to be able to achieve the great things I achieve – to get it all done!

I have become an incredibly productive human not because I'm smarter or faster, but because I love systems. I love science and data. And actually, I don't simply rely on intelligence. I believe that attitude and effort trumps intelligence every day and in every way, and I see evidence for this everywhere.

Quite simply, in my business and life I use science and systems in order to get what I want – and as I often say, what I want is at the heart of what most humans want. It's purpose and joy. The strategic bookkeeper gives me a purpose in life only second to being a mother, and I could only have built my little empire by becoming a highly productive human.

So what are my secrets of time architecture and productivity? They're as easy as counting to five.

1. I use the science of 'when'.
2. I am a proactive, not distracted, single tasker.
3. I work with the law of polarity.
4. I am all about habits – KISS.
5. I turn up as a leader and a manager with no apologies.

These five points, my friends, are the basis of my primary productivity time-architecture and they all work together like a well-oiled machine.

Here's how you can use these five points to create your own time architecture and get 10 times more done – which is how you'll get it all done!

Part one – The Science of When.
Here again, I am building on a foundation of knowledge gathered and shared by another great mind – in this case Daniel Pink. His book, simply called *When*, is a fantastic eye-opener. He talks about the science of timing, and how to make it a part of your everyday life. And this isn't just his great idea – his research encompasses a range of disciplines from economics to biology and psychology.

Daniel's research is why elective surgery is usually scheduled for the morning, and it's why I call my morning brain my surgeon's brain. You see, his research has determined that 80% of us function best in the morning, we're called larks and birds. The remaining 20 percent of us are *night owls*. Owl body clocks are set to stay up late and to sleep late, and they function at their peak in the evening - the opposite to the rest of us.

Now, I feel for night owls because they get a bad rap but the point is, what every one of us has to work out is which perch we sit on – whether we are larks, birds or night owls – and figure out when our minds are at their best. And if night owls are firing while the rest of us are sleeping, good luck to them.

Your brain's best functioning time is your biggest opportunity to get into "the flow state" also known as *the golden hour,* when you'll have your best ideas and can do your best work.

I'm a bird, and I feel fortunate to function best with the majority, it makes life a bit easier. Winning! Whatever your natural rhythm, find it and use it. That's what I do, and it means that I'm always feeling my best when I want to work most effectively.

The way I use the *science of when* is combined with all the other steps and so I'll first explain them, and then I'll illustrate what I do in order to help you become a productivity ninja.

Productivity tip: listen to the summary of "When" on the blinkist app (or another summary app)

Part two – Be a Proactive (not distracted) Single Tasker.
Following on from the science of when, in this part 2, I want to show you how to...

1. Stop checking your email before 11am
2. A word on how to handle email
3. Make distractions invisible (like atomic habits teaches you)
4. Plan
5. Single task

This looks like a bit of a 5-point plan, right? Systems, yes!

Now, because all this "getting it done" stuff around mindset and productivity really is the doorway to success (to make the mechanics work) I recommend that you make it visual (think back of the toilet door and on your desk), and bed it down into habit.

To help you nail this 5-point plan, let me illustrate the first thing you might be doing wrong that sets off a chain reaction. You see, in my experience, *your normal day* probably begins with checking your email.

This fatal mistake is like a domino that sets off the chain reaction, not to mention you're using your surgeon's brain to do mundane tasks.

Then, by the time your surgeon's brain has expired, you're ready to work on your business - oh-oh, it's too late! Cue the "where was I" feeling.

By now, you're deep in reactive, distracted, multitasker mode, and with the golden hours behind you, the best you can do is go on to client work - more stuff you could do with your hands tied behind your back. *This is the norm.*

My advice to you is - *don't be normal!*

Bookkeepers love email, which makes sense given that the majority of us are introverts and administrators, which naturally makes us happy behind a keyboard - we have good literacy skills and speed typing skills.

We'll revisit that in the last chapter when we discuss "communication as a secret marketing weapon" and, the fact that your clients aren't the same as you and therefore, you need to get out from behind your email and be smarter around how you communicate with them.

In terms of productivity

1. It's just another in-box
2. Email is not your agenda - it's everyone else's (cue: react!)
3. Email tennis is a sport where everyone loses
4. Email, particularly if you're using it to send text (rather than voice clips) is one of the least user-friendly forms of communication (in a world where we have so many ways to communicate)
5. It's a monologue

I'm not going to elaborate any further on these 5 points but rather, ask you to think on them. If you'd like me to elaborate, shoot me an email and request a podcast - you might even try sending me a voice clip using tech like otter.ai or veed.io.

Your brain has three parts to it

- Fight or flight
- Reactive
- Proactive

...which you can see Illustrated on a brain model you can access at https://www.thestrategicbookkeeper.global/BluePrintResources

You know fight-or-flight—it's the primal part of our brain that helps us survive. Most psychologists would give the example of its origin, helping us get up and run away from the sabre-tooth tiger.

These days, we don't use that part of our brain as much, and so we've evolved into a more general reactive mode.

While being reactive will always serve in some way, we need to evolve further and build the proactive part of our brain, which I've also heard described as the empire-builder brain, something I've worked hard on since learning this.

Unfortunately, this is harder than you might think because our lives and our environment are set up to make us reactive, distracted, multi-taskers. Our kids, our phones, everything around us is distracting us, making us react, making us do multiple things at once.

And of course, we need to react and to multi-task some of the time, for primary survival. Our biology, our bodies are literally built to react. Think about breastfeeding. You have no choice – your baby cries and your body literally reacts by producing milk.

But just as there's a time to be reactive and to meet the challenges of the current situation by multitasking, there's a time to consciously put reactivity aside and focus deeply on the task at hand. To say to yourself, *No, I am not going to stop every time my phone rings or an email comes through, or try and cook and clean while I work on this file. That stuff will wait, and my brain is telling me to react to it because that's the way it's always worked. So just focus, get this job done, and then go do that other stuff.*

Learning to stop reacting 100 percent of the time and become a proactive, not distracted single tasker is hard because this stuff is hardwired into us, but the rewards are incredible. You'll get complex and challenging things done, your powers of concentration will increase, and your clients will be happier.

So, how to nail the 5-point plan I gave you a moment ago?

KISS - Keep it super simple. Make it all habit!

Step 3: Work with the Law of Polarity.

Polarity is really about opposites. It's a simple yet powerful, real law (like gravity) that you can learn and use to assist you to become a highly productive human in your business and personal life. It works like this: every time you say *yes* to something you say *no* to something else. When you say *yes* to going to sleep you say *no* to being awake. When you say *yes* to checking your email, you say *no* to continuing to concentrate on what you're doing.

Every time you say yes to an item on your to-do list, or to picking up an activity, or whatever, you are unconsciously (or maybe sometimes consciously) saying no to something else that you can't do in that time.

This is science, and I love science.

I use this simple yet mighty truth on steroids, my friends. In terms of what's on your to-do list you can a) do it b) delegate it, or c) don't do it.

Each one of these has a value but in my experience, I've found that the most powerful and liberating of all three is *don't do it*. After that comes *delegate*, and my least used of all is *do it*.

I know that sounds counterintuitive, and I can hear you saying, "why Jeannie?" But there's another principle at play here, and that is, be extra picky about what you're saying *yes* to.

Time wealth is something I value so highly that I've become a little bit obsessed with trying to find and do only the 5 percent of all the things that will give me 95 percent of the result. Why plough through every little thing I might do – the 95 percent that might move the needle a fraction? My time is too precious to put into an activity that gives me a tiny little result – and the alternative things I might do with that time are far, far too enjoyable.

I want a big bang for my time buck and this is one of the big things that I would love to inspire bookkeepers to become a little bit obsessed with as well. There's no doubt that time and money are the two big things that we want and need to pull out of our businesses. There tends to be a natural focus on money but the idea that the time would simply come with it is just not true.

You need to learn how to make time just like you learn how to make money.

Working with the Law of Polarity.
Polarity is one of the seven laws of alchemy. In my business and absolutely in my personal life too, I remind myself that when I say *yes* to one thing I'm saying *no* to another. When you're aware that you're making a choice to do one thing and not another, you tend to weigh the options more carefully. What is the value of each to you?

The law of polarity is intrinsically linked to the other concepts I'm explaining here in getting it done – it's about focusing on the five percent activities and not doing the 95 percent activities. How do you recognise which is the five percent activity that yields the best return? You slow down and stop. You make room for your brain and your body to see and do things differently.

You only have each moment, and you can only do what you are doing in the moment. Therefore, you can't do what you are not doing in the moment. This might sound a bit ethereal or even spiritual and perhaps it is.

It's not my intention to go too deeply into how I use polarity, just to give you the headlines. But please understand, it's part of my BluePrint, and it's important that you understand the Law of Polarity and use it the way it's intended. The bookkeepers inside my Transformation Program, who do all the things step-by-step, who use the BluePrint just as it is and don't mess with it, they are the other ones that get the biggest results - as a rule, that's generating 6 figures in a year.

What I want you to avoid is making yourself busy with a whole lot of things to the point where things are so hectic you don't realise all the things you are not doing. Because bookkeepers tend to do that, and it's definitely what contributes to nine out of ten of them never finding the success they're looking for.

Planning with Polarity.
One of the ways I've learned to harness the power of polarity is to use my time more effectively in planning before acting. The polar opposite of planning is the not so subtle art of throwing sh*t at a wall and hoping it sticks.

For example, imagine going on Facebook, maybe joining a few business groups, and then posting about your business on their pages with the idea that you're doing 'marketing' - going down the rabbit hole of creating Canva posts, and adding stuff that's just ad hoc, that isn't backed up by an overarching strategic plan. That's not marketing. It's throwing sh*t at a wall and hoping it sticks. Like a hamster on a wheel, he's running fast but he's busy going nowhere and he's proudly telling himself he has great traction.

When you throw sh*t at a wall like this, eventually you might get some results, but you've invested 95 percent of your time and money for a (maybe) 5 percent result. Sure, when you get a result it gives your ego a bit of a boost because let's face it, you've just invested a lot of your business and personal time into these activities and you want to believe that you know a bit about marketing. But all I see is a bookkeeper ending up just like that hamster on a wheel – busy, busy, busy but the numbers are just not adding up at the end of the day. And it's perpetual.

The broken-down car.

Another way of looking at it is to imagine your business speeding down the highway like a broken car. You're blowing smoke and burning oil and sooner or later something is going to give and you know it, but with the wheels in motion, speeding down the highway, you don't know how to find the time to actually fix it.

We use the car analogy a lot in my Transformation Program and my tribe and I laugh as we all relate to it. I too once had the broken down car flying down the highway. I was once scratching my head wondering how the hell I'd fix it while the wheels were spinning – the business going full steam ahead but the vehicle itself was in danger of total breakdown.

Here's the thing. Eighty percent of the bookkeepers who join my program have a car that needs to be fixed. Twenty percent are at startup stage with the opportunity to build a Ferrari before they put it on the road. The thing they have in common is that quite honestly 100 percent of them will need to give me the hours, the attitude and follow the system I give them. I can't say it's easier for one than the other but knowing and understanding where you are is helpful.

Do you know which one you are? Is your bookkeeping car speeding down the highway in desperate need of being fixed, or are you ready to build a Ferrari?

I can help.
Either way, the solution is to press pause, take a breath, and come back to strategy. Learn the BluePrint and implement it and resist the temptation to throw sh*t at a wall. Sure, it can be a bit of fun – trust me, from time to time I do it too. I busy myself with activities that feel like they give me the result, and sometimes they even do, but it's not the right result. It's not a sustainable result. It's not a repeatable result. And like you, I get lost when I go down that rabbit hole because the truth is, when you say *yes* to throwing sh*t at a wall, you're saying *no* to significant, repeatable, sustainable strategic results.

The absolute key takeaway from the Law of Polarity that I want for you right now is this... trust me now and believe me later, I've been there done that. But then I spent four years and hundreds of thousands of dollars testing and perfecting everything so that I could give you the BluePrint. I can genuinely help you.

Don't go rogue on me – say *no* to anything outside the BluePrint so that you have room to say *yes* to what the BluePrint and what I can do for you.

Step 4: Habits (KISS)

Here's a riddle.

I am your constant companion.

I am your greatest helper or heaviest burden.

I will push you onward or drag you down to failure.

I am completely at your command.

Half of the things you do, you might as well turn over to me and I will do them quickly and correctly.

I am easily managed but you must be firm with me.

Show me exactly how you want something done and after a few lessons I will do it automatically.

I am the servant of great people, and alas, of all failures as well.

Those who are great, I have made great.

Those who are failures, I have made failures.

I am not a machine, though I work with the precision of a machine plus the intelligence of a person.

You may run me for profit or run me for ruin - it makes no difference to me.

Take me, train me, be firm with me, and I will place the world at your feet.

Be easy with me and I will destroy you.

Who am I? I am Habit.

Humans are lazy and not very disciplined and easily distracted. But there's an extraordinarily easy solution: Keep It Super Simple (KISS). And the best way to do that is not to try and muscle your way to success, but to let the most powerful organ in your body, your brain, do all the heavy lifting without you even noticing. Train yourself to use systems and let the machine of habit take over.

Read Atomic Habits.
Atomic Habits is a book by the author James Clear, and the subtitle is *Tiny changes, remarkable results*. When I first read it, I learned that I was already doing a lot of the things

James recommends, because I love systems. My partner laughs that I have little systems in everything I do. But for so many of the bookkeepers I meet and who are in my tribe, the beautiful systems James Clear has crafted in his book are a mind-bending revelation.

A lot of what I'm illustrating here to help you get it done are examples of the little systems I use. Regularly I'm told how smart I am, how I'm super human and even how I'm an alien, but take away my systems, take away my BluePrint and I think perhaps you'd be taking away a good deal of my power.

You can harness this power for yourself by leaning into *Atomic Habits*, because what James Clear teaches is absolutely part of making the BluePrint work for you.

Step 4: Lead and Manage – No Apologies.

Part of the BluePrint is stepping up as an unapologetic leader and manager. I talk about this in my first book, so I won't go on about it too much here. But I strongly recommend that you read my first book, *The Strategic Bookkeeper* and in particular the last two chapters, *The Beauty of Systems* and *The Strength of Teams*.

I call unapologetic leadership and management being an *A Leader* and an *A Manager*. And being these things is how you build and cultivate an *A Team*. If you're not an *A Leader* and an *A Manager,* you're most likely a people pleasing leader/manager. Being a people pleaser in your business will lead you to becoming a *B Leader/ Manager*, and that will end up by cultivating a time and joy-sucking *B Team* that will damage your brand, your business, your clients and your sanity. And trust me, you do not want to be saddled with that.

So, to recap, go back to *The Strategic Bookkeeper* to learn more about becoming an *A Leader* and an *A Manager*. See how my books work together now?

A summary.

Before we move on to the *Mechanics* part of *Getting It Done,* a note on what I've shared so far, and what your homework needs to be.

Once again, I could write an entire book on mindset and productivity and in this book I'm giving you more of the headlines and less of the detail. In order to help you with some of the concepts I'm sharing around mindset and productivity, here's what I recommend you do.

Go on a journey that involves the 3 A's to change:

1. Awareness
2. Acceptance
3. Action.

For the next few weeks in your business, put yourself into the Awareness phase. Keep this book with you, maybe listen to the audiobook, rinsing and repeating on the mindset and productivity parts, and sit in an Awareness of what you're doing compared to what I'm suggesting.

Look at what you're doing right now versus what you need to be doing, and in particular, try to be aware of what you are saying *yes* to and what you're saying *no* to, in terms of:

- Are you using the Science of When?
- Are you being a Proactive Not-Distracted Single Tasker, working on your business using an overarching strategy – a BluePrint?
- Are you working with the Law of Polarity?
- Are you cultivating Habits and Keeping It Simple?

Or are you simply reacting to all the noise around you including your email and your phone?

Are you busy with all the things that come at you, or are you creating space by saying *no* and simply not doing a whole lot of stuff but rather doing the five percent based on your BluePrint?

Are you beating yourself up for not being more disciplined, or are you using Atomic Habits? Adopting really smart but easy disciplines like putting your phone in another other room, and not looking at your email at all until midday?

Are you being a people pleaser, or have you decided on your agenda – to become determined to hold the people around you accountable to it?

On that last one... in my private life I am an absolute marshmallow. A big softie and dare I it say, easy to take advantage of. But in my business life, since deciding I must show up as an A Leader and Manager, I could be mistaken occasionally for being a little rude or even offensive.

Now, I do my best to always be well-mannered, but I am clear, I'm direct, I know the direction my ship is heading, and I know what my team needs to do to take us to the destination. So I do it, habitually and unapologetically.

I say "no" a lot.

And that, my friends, is a big part of the BluePrint and how I've created success in every area of my business and my personal life. And let me tell you right now, it's worth stepping up for.

Step 3: The Mechanics.

Okay, you've learned how mindset and productivity are essential to success and you now know the importance of mastering these. They're mostly about the way you think and plan. They're kind of philosophical in nature. But the third part of this chapter is all about the mechanics – things you need to do and build to find success in your bookkeeping practice.

Now I think of the mechanics as simple – but remember, simple doesn't necessarily mean easy!

If you've read my first book – and I truly hope you have – and you've come this far in this book, you'll know that a lot of what I teach *is* the mechanics. The BluePrint is essentially a graphic representation of the mechanics of getting it done and becoming a strategic bookkeeper. My weekly podcast primarily goes into the mechanics and occasionally into mindset and productivity. My tribe spends a lot of their time concentrating on getting the mechanics right. Because, like anything mechanical, it's about repetition.

They say you get to be a sports pro by spending 10,000 hours practising your shots, your moves or whatever. Well, I'm way past 10,000 hours now, and that's why I'm a pro at everything you see on the BluePrint – and that's what I want for you.

I'm here for you.
So much of your success turns on getting the mechanical actions right, and it can be tough to get/do sometimes. So when you're working through this chapter, remember you can email me with your questions any time. If I don't answer you directly, I'll more than likely devote an episode of my podcast to your issue.

The BluePrint.

As you're by now well aware, the BluePrint is your roadmap to getting both the mental and physical aspects of the job right – nailing the philosophical as well as the mechanical. And in the rest of this book we'll be working to nail down the mechanics.

Financial Management.
If you look at the BluePrint you'll see that this is the next item on the list.

When I reflect on my journey as a bookkeeper in practice and when I look at the experiences of my tribe members - in terms of financial management, there is one main thing, one word, one trigger, one cost with the potential to bring us undone.

Staff.

Why do you say that, Jeannie? I hear you ask.

And there are three possibly disastrous effects of making big staffing mistakes.

- Budget blowouts.
- The wrong people in the wrong places.
- Bigger is not better.

Let's take a look at these three dangers to your business.

Budget blowouts

Budget blowouts can be avoided by learning to carefully manage the budgeted time allocation for each job – tracking the time spent on the job, which is the "actual" time spent (versus budget).

Use a traffic light system to identify any actual job times that exceed the budget and work out why. Hint: either the volume of work has increased, or the staff member is not efficient enough.

If the volume has increased this can be easily rectified by re-scoping and repackaging into a new service level agreement for your client. If it's the staff member, they need to be retrained or let go.

In my signature program, the *done-for-you standard operating procedures* gives you a budget versus actual spreadsheet which we teach you to use.

If you're joining my program please remember we've spent over a decade perfecting all this so please, simply follow the system and let the magic happen (rather than trying to reinvent the wheel).

One of our tribe members, Michelle– who runs a highly successful bookkeeping practice – identified that through learning and implementing our standard operating procedures she could likely double her gross profit. Just like Michelle you need to invest in nailing the financial management of your bookkeeping practice.

The wrong people in the wrong places.

This is a little trickier because while this sometimes happens due to a lack of education or experience, it can also happen due to people-pleasing / nice guy management. And as you know, I've been there done that!

You need to ensure that you put the right people in the right places. And as I explained in my first book, that means being an A leader and an A manager – and that's non-negotiable.

In our program we share a BluePrint for how to recruit and manage your team to nail the financial management of your bookkeeping practice which I developed over about 13 years of learning by failing - so you can avoid the same mistakes.

Kelly's Story.

Kelly's story is a somewhat common tale inside my program. When she joined my program Kelly was a solo operator, and she'd only just began as a bookkeeper in practice working for herself.

She was living off her savings when she joined my program, but a year later she had a six figure income and a 12-week wait list. With a growing client list and a need for the right people in the right jobs, it was a natural for Kelly to get my help to implement our recruitment system.

At the time of writing this book she has her head down and bum up as she onboards her first team member, knowing that the financial management of her bookkeeping practice is safe and sound because she's using my tried and true system. If you'd like me to help you through this challenge, shoot me an email – I'd love to help.

Rinse and repeat.

I'm going to stay on this for just a minute longer because as I write this I'm imagining bookkeepers everywhere sitting at their desks head down bum up, with a dream in their heart that they'll build the business, the income, the time, the purpose and the joy they desire.

But it's so easy to expand your team, your client list and your own workload without getting any of those wonderful benefits. To become bigger, but not better.

This is where having the mechanics that I have designed, tested and proven can make a huge difference. Mistakes around staffing can cost you money and destroy your peace of mind. I see bookkeepers getting this wrong every day and every day it breaks my heart.

I want you to get it right, and honestly, the best way I can help you is inside my signature program, so I encourage you to join our priority list at https://www.the strategicbookkeeper.global/tsb.

Okay, now it's time to get right down to the reason we're all here – working through the BluePrint that will transform your business and help you become a happy strategic bookkeeper enjoying the time and financial wealth you deserve. Let's go!

Chapter 3 - Your Foundation.

The BluePrint is, if I say so myself, a beautiful piece of work. It's balanced, it has flow and logic, and above all it's elegantly simple. So now it's time to dissect it and start learning how to implement each of its elements. Just a reminder that a lot of the elements of the BluePrint are covered in more detail in my first book, *The Strategic Bookkeeper*, so if you haven't followed my advice and gone back to read (or re-read) that first, I suggest you do so now. It's okay, I'll wait.

Your Plan.

When you look at the BluePrint, you'll see that at the top left I have noted all the elements of creating a Foundation. The good news is, we've already covered Team, Mindset and Productivity, and as noted above, the section on Branding is comprehensively discussed in my first book, *The Strategic Bookkeeper*. You knew that because you've already read it, right?

So that leaves the crucial cornerstone of your Foundation, your Plan.

So let's talk about creating a basic but powerful plan. A bookkeeper reached out to me the other day, let's call her Sally. Sally is inside my Starter Membership and she's going to join my Program next. That's relevant because it changes the process she needs to follow to get it right and the team she has to recruit to do it.

Sally had some great questions, and one of them was *should I create a business plan?* She also asked if there were things in terms of planning she shouldn't bother doing based on what she would get in the Program.

The answer to both questions was a resounding *Yes*.

To begin with, if you're planning on joining my Program, you don't need to worry too much about a lot of the planning – although it's still required, we'll help you with a lot of it, and you'll benefit from our years of experience.

Your Business Playbook.

The first thing to do is create a document called *My Business Playbook*. You are absolutely going to need to plan to build out everything on the BluePrint, and this is where you'll keep all of the information you need.

In your book resources which you can access at https://www.thestrategicbookkeeper.global/BluePrintResources

I've given you a my-business-playbook template. Hot tip; this doubles as an advisory resource for your clients. You're welcome (wink).

If you are joining my Program all that building out will be done for you or with you, but whether you're joining us or not you'll need to start with your *Business Playbook*. It's an incredibly powerful tool and reference, and I only wish someone had shown me something like this at the beginning of my bookkeeping practice journey. It would have saved me a lot of time, mistakes and heartaches!

Setting up your *Business Playbook* is quite simple, as it involves setting some basic goals around your income, your time and your first technical hire.

Napkin (North Star) numbers.
Let's start with your goals around earnings. I call these napkin numbers because rather than create spreadsheets and detailed numbers around revenue, cost of sales, operational costs and so on, in my experience it's easier to just jot down a basic set of numbers that you can think of as destination points. Another way of thinking of these numbers is that they represent your goals that you can use to work backwards – to break down what you need to get there. So you can also call them North Star numbers.

Napkin/North Star numbers don't need to be super accurate or anything – you can jot them down on a napkin to begin with and refine and adjust later if necessary. That's why they're also napkin numbers.

If you're already a bookkeeper in practice you can use this exercise to do a bit of a now/future analysis. Look at your profit and loss and where you are now, and then start again with these napkin numbers. When you have both sets of numbers in front of you, you can quickly and easily see what needs to be done to renovate your profit and loss and set your bookkeeping practice in the right direction.

Usually that's a combination of building and implementing many things on the Bookkeeping Practice BluePrint.

I meet a lot of bookkeepers in practice whose revenue is going up and up but what they're taking home, their time wealth is not. The BluePrint will give you the tools to ensure that you don't fall into that trap. I want to help you create what I've created – a business that's financially very attractive for me, but maybe more importantly, gives me the time I need to enjoy my financial freedom.

Lessons from the tribe.

Let's go back to our friend Sally, who I mentioned above. I'm going to tell you what I told Sally who's in startup mode and will be a solo operator in the early days. Don't forget, Sally will be joining my Program, so her level of workload and responsibility for planning and building will be different to yours if you are going it alone. We'll be there with Sally every step of the way, adding our skillsets and experience to her ideas and aspirations.

Income.

First, work out how much income you want to earn within the first six months of commencing your bookkeeping practice. This will be different for everyone based on your situation and financial requirements.

Sally wants to create revenue of a hundred thousand dollars per annum within six months. As a sole operator we can assume a third of that will go to the cost of running her business, so she will be able to take $66,000 a year as a starting income within six months.

Beyond that, Sally wants to aim for our bookkeeping practice BluePrint sweet spot, which is $200,000 take home income – and she wants to achieve that within two years.

Busy not thriving.

To achieve her first goal of $100,000 revenue within six months what does Sally do? This, my friends, is the critical part of your napkin numbers planning.

When I started in practice I simply provided my services for a fee, thinking that if I kept doing that, eventually I'd get busy and I'd be making lots of money so I'd be able to live the lifestyle I went into it for in the first place, right?

Wrong. Critical mistake – because what I built at that time was *busy not thriving.* And every day, I hear from bookkeepers who tell me they are off-the-charts busy but they hate what they do now. I could go on about this but I've made a commitment to keep this book short and really punchy. How am I doing?

There's something that the tribe inside my Program embrace when I say it, and that is *trust me now believe me later*, and in this book I'm absolutely going to ask you to do that.

I've been there done that, and I'm helping bookkeepers all over the world knock it out of the ballpark. Trust me now believe me later, that formula I used early on, it doesn't work. If you're using it, stop it and do the following.

Rather than simply taking on work to try and build your $100,000 of revenue (or whatever your target is) in the first six months, you should be far more strategic. If I had my time over again, that's exactly what I would do and that's why I want to share my experience with you – to stop you from making the mistakes I made.

Eventually, I stopped trying to increase my *volume* of clients and decided to target a smaller number of clients paying a much higher fee. The numbers here can be super simple – 10 clients paying you an average of $10,000 a year. But let's break that down even further.

You aim for 10 clients paying you an average of $200 a week, which works out to about an hour and a half of technical bookkeeping. In addition, you provide these clients with a monthly advisory meeting, so you can investigate the numbers with them.

That works out to just shy of 18 hours per week on the technical bookkeeping and advisory side to achieve that first goal of $100,000 revenue and $66,000 dollars net profit.

Now, a lot of bookkeepers will serve more like 30 clients to achieve that kind of revenue and end up putting in two to three times the hours in Sally's example. That tends to lead to them employing people, and the result for them is high revenue, low profit – and no time.

Doing these napkin numbers and having a real plan like this gives you the clarity to see what you really need to do to build *thriving* rather than *busy*.

Do your napkin numbers now or read this book right through, then circle back and do it on your second read. But do them.

Time.
Nothing is more precious than time. One of the most beautiful things about my life now is that I've earned the time to spend enjoying the financial success I've achieved. But that didn't come easily or quickly. I'm not going to lie, there are times in your bookkeeping practice journey when you are going to need to buckle down and put in the ***hours and the attitude.***

You're going to have to put your head down, work hard and work smart and you're probably going to feel uncomfortable.

A tribal story.

Kelly joined my Program in August 2023, soon after I opened the doors for the first time. At first she was reluctant as she'd had a bookkeeping coach before but it didn't work out. I actually suggested Kelly consider not joining my Program, as I was worried about the baggage from that relationship affecting her ability to trust me. Funnily enough that was the wake up call she needed to just do it.

When she joined my Program, Kelly was living off her savings. A year later her take home pay was $125,000 per annum. In a moment I'll tell you how she did that, but right now what I want to tell you is related to hours and attitude. Because Kelly absolutely felt a lot of discomfort – dare I say pain – on the way to achieving her goal.

She got so busy that when we caught up recently, we talked about her deviating from our regular waitlist process to simply saying to prospective clients *Sorry I probably can't work with you for 12 weeks.*

Interestingly, after Kelly and I decided on that approach to the waitlist she called me back later that day to tell me two more prospective clients had called, and she'd delivered the *Sorry* speech to them. To her delight, they both were adamant that they'd be happy to wait because they were both 100 percent sure that she was the Strategic Bookkeeper they wanted and needed. Competitive advantage much? Boom.

At that point I worked on getting her a full-time all-rounder, a bookkeeper who could do the technical work plus all the general and marketing and practice administration.

I told Kelly then what I'll tell you now... pain proceeds victory. Lean in.

The reward of time will come on the other side of the pain – after we get together to truly scale your bookkeeping practice, but first we have to tame the rest of the BluePrint, okay?

Of course that wasn't the only secret to Kelly's success. She did what every successful tribe member inside my Program does: she implemented everything step-by-step, she refined her marketing to ensure she got the nuances right, and most importantly she didn't go rogue on me or do anything outside of my Program.

Be like Kelly – trust me now and you'll believe me later.

I have already tested every strategy known to man to come up with the five percent of things you need to do to get 95% of the result. I've built all the world-class assets and collateral you need which includes a huge array of

THE
BOOKKEEPING PRACTICE
BLUEPRINT

powerful marketing copywriting. I've already built the competitive advantage that leads to that wait list result for you.

Doing your napkin numbers on time looks like this.

We've established that there's a period of pain, discomfort, effort and attitude. But what happens after that? How much time do you want to spend working and how much time do you want off? Write it down on your napkin.

I asked Kelly to plan when she would like to hire a full-time bookkeeper to sacrifice some income for time – time both for herself and to work on the business.

Let's look at her napkin numbers. If Kelly gets to that one hundred thousand revenue goal, giving her approximately $66,000 take-home pay as a solo operator, she'll need to reserve about 30,000 a year for that full-time person with the way that we recruit.

Now, early on in my practice, my then husband had pivoted to being the main breadwinner, which meant that I could sacrifice some income a little earlier to buy the time to spend working on my business to scale it. And you can absolutely choose to do the same thing, to sacrifice income earlier on if that's possible and if that's what you want.

Or you can set a goal to build more revenue before you do that. Just do your napkin numbers on time, and consider when you'll be able to make your first technical hire.

And remember, these are not 'set and forget' goals. I recommend revisiting them regularly and thinking about them a lot. These napkin numbers are your North Star, and they should dictate how you show up and who you bring on as clients.

To rinse and repeat for a minute, if your strategy is to simply bring on work and build a busy practice, you will build a broken practice which unfortunately is what nine out of 10 bookkeepers do. That's why a plan is so critical. It's your roadmap to success, as well as the first pillar of the BluePrint.

Your Brand.

Everyone knows how important a brand is to success these days. No brand, no name, no future. That's why Brand is so high on the BluePrint structure. But I don't intend to go over old ground here. If you haven't read my first book, *The Strategic Bookkeeper*, I'm going to direct you back to that now – there's an entire chapter on brand and a brand-building Playbook in there.

In the interest of only giving you new information here, I'm not going to rinse and repeat on that right now. I'm going to make the assumption that you're happy to press pause on this book and read or listen to my first book first, which you'll find on my website.

I do want to say that brand alone won't build the business of your dreams but without the right brand in place, you won't get there either. It's definitely a big part of the foundation of your house, but you still need to build the house, put the windows and doors in all the other parts of the BluePrint.

Having an on-point brand that does the talking for you gives you a competitive advantage. Remember Kelly and how her prospective clients were prepared to wait three months to work with her even though she charges a lot more than average? That's the power of brand when it's used with all the other parts of your BluePrint.

A note on assets.

If you're not joining my program please look at the BluePrint now and you'll see the three foundational brand assets to build and get working in your practice – your signature brochure, your social media and your website.

You can use my first book to learn about and build your brand – please note that it's important to include your menu in your signature brochure, and I explain all that in *The Strategic Bookkeeper* and provide you with a workbook so you can do it yourself.

If you're joining my program all the work around brand is done for you – your brochure, your social media and everything you need to get a world-class website done in days.

One of the reasons that the *done for you* brand that we'll work with you to create inside my program works so well, is because your signature brochure, your social media and your website material are built on rock solid strategy such as the Six Pillars of Persuasion.

The Six Pillars of Persuasion.

While the Six Pillars of Persuasion are sometimes considered 'old school' principles, I base my application of them on Robert Cialdini's book *Influence: The Psychology of Persuasion*, and I swear by them - because they work. This is science, and you know I love science.

Let's take a look at Six Pillars now so that you can try weaving them through your brand foundations:

1. Reciprocity:
Think Tupperware: everybody gets a gift. Giving creates persuasion as we are hard-wired to reciprocate. Looking at the BluePrint, the best example of reciprocation you can use in your bookkeeping practice is your welcome line nurture assets inside your product ladder (don't worry, there's a chapter on the Product Ladder).

Basically, these are gifts you give away to anyone and everyone. For example, inside the Program we teach you how to deliver business fundamentals training, a business health check, a future analysis, and a few more things that you can give away to your prospective clients and your clients. Including a co-authored eBook 'How to' guide.

This will all make more sense as we go on, the key takeaway for you right now is that reciprocation is about giving something away as the first pillar of persuasion.

2. Scarcity.
Remember the waitlist story with Kelly? When something is scarce, we're hard-wired to see this as proof that it's valuable and want it more than ever.

Scarcity inside your bookkeeping practice is simple. You have limited capacity, and you need to make sure that everybody knows about that. My tribe tell me that when they introduce scarcity into the conversion process it absolutely changes the game for them.

During an implementation coaching session I dove deeper into this and one of our tribe, Diane, immediately sent a prospective client a text message. She was following up on a proposal that had been sent out for signing for a month, and she said, "Hi Tom, I'm just touching base as a courtesy as we are just about to go to waitlist and I don't want you to miss out on having your books brought up to date. Remember, I'm just a phone call away if you have any questions. Chat soon."

Tom had let it slide for a month, but mention of being waitlisted spurred him to action and he signed right there and then. What a fantastic result for Diane and a brilliant example of the power of scarcity.

3. Authority.
This is one we can all relate to – we are hard-wired to make quicker decisions when an expert or authority is talking to us.

In my first book I give you everything you need to build your profile as an authority. The trick is to ensure you put that authority on prominent display in all your brand and marketing collateral and throughout your sales process.

4. Commitment and consistency.
I love this one. Humans are far more likely to continue with their commitment consistently, meaning once they take one buying step, they are more likely to keep moving in the same direction.

Once again, I'll explain what we're doing inside the Program so you can recreate it if you're not joining my tribe. We use 10 key Welcome Line Nurture Assets, which range from no cost to low cost. These assets include things like low cost file health checks, low cost business health checks, a now/future analysis session, and even a *7 Deadly Sins* eBook. There's more on this inside the *Your Product Ladder* chapter, coming up soon.

Each prospective client takes advantage of two or more of these assets before they make their first major purchase, and then again before they commit to $10,000 or more in annual services. To me, the really interesting thing here is that the hardest sale you'll ever make is $100, and the easiest sale you'll make is $10,000.

That's just how Commitment and Consistency works. Your clients will make a faster and more confident decision on a high ticket purchase after they've taken multiple steps in that direction already, by engaging in the nurturing assets you've provided.

5. Liking.
Here's another one that sounds like common sense but is actually a deep insight to take

on board: people are more likely to buy from people they like.

Thanks Jeannie, I understand that, but how do I make it work for me? I can hear you asking. Easy. You level up the way you communicate with your clients. Get out from behind that keyboard and pick up the phone. Stop having monologues via email and have actual dialogues with your clients. Be friendly. Be helpful. Be responsive. Listen, and act.

Above all, make sure that you've got the marketing X Factor, which is trust – do what you said you would do in the timeframe you said you'd do it, no excuses. It sounds so simple, but I see bookkeepers fail at this all the time. I move heaven and earth to keep my promises and so should you.

6. Consensus.
I think the better name for this one is social proof. Humans will buy products or services when they see that they are popular. They see that happening and they come to the conclusion that the consensus opinion must be right – those products or services must be worth buying.

To put the pillar of Consensus to work for you, make sure your results are visible. Get clients to give you Google reviews and display them throughout your brand foundations.

That's the Six Pillars.

Using these six pillars together in all your Brand, marketing and sales collateral and processes, is how you'll help your market make the decision to choose you without price as a priority – just like Kelly.

Understanding and using these six pillars will win you the step-by-step attention of your market to attract prospective clients, make them clients, and then grow them into VIPs.

If you don't get the Six Pillars right you'll be a lot like this enthusiastic inventor.

Once upon a time, a young entrepreneur had an idea for a piece of revolutionary exercise equipment. Just like you, he had a dream in his heart, to bring an extraordinary product to the market. His was called the V-Bar.

Now there is no doubt that just like your bookkeeping service, the V-Bar was top notch and the young entrepreneur invested time and money into taking it to market. But no matter how hard he tried he couldn't sell a unit. Regardless of how good the product was, nobody would buy it.

His business dream quickly became a nightmare and so he decided to sell the V-Bar, along with all the rights, to another entrepreneur. That entrepreneur went on to make the V-Bar the best-selling piece of exercise equipment ever made.

You know it as the Thigh Master. Same product, different pitch. Same product better persuasion. You can bet your bottom dollar the six pillars of persuasion were at work in every single part of the brand, marketing, and the selling collateral and processes attached to the Thigh Master.

The moral here is that your ability to deliver a world-class bookkeeping service will go unnoticed if you're unable to sell that service. So please, if you only take one thing away from this book, make it that you need to learn the language of persuasion.

The Why of Persuasion.

Now I won't lie to you, being a master of persuasion is not what most bookkeepers are built for. In fact it's often their primary weakness. I'm going to be honest – I'm really good at this stuff. I was raised by an accountant mother and a sales marketing guru father, and I ended up a management accountant (now The Strategic Bookkeeper) who specialises in sales and marketing. Go figure.

But I know I am a bit of a unicorn. Most bookkeepers are not naturals at this and that's why I've spent a lot of time, money and effort building a program that would serve them up everything they needed to hit the ground running so they could get results ahead of fully understanding all the ins and outs.

I just realised that if I was going to do what most bookkeeping coaches do, which is to try and teach bookkeepers to be sales and marketing specialists, it would take a long time and a lot of money. And I know that bookkeepers need to get results fast.

Any money you invest in growing your bookkeeping practice needs to be returned in results – fast. So I built my whole system to deliver results first and foremost, and I'm thrilled to say it's working. A lot of my tribe members tell me that they are getting results using the tools before they fully understand everything about them. It's what I call my crazy science method, but I think it's logical. I specialise in what I'm really good at, which is brand marketing and selling, and you leverage my zone of genius.

Remember I said you won't win the game without a winning team, sitting in your zone of genius and surrounding yourself with a team that complements you is at the heart and soul of that.

The How of Persuasion.

I recommend that you type these Six Pillars of Persuasion up, print them out, and actually use them as you create your brand foundations and all your other brand, marketing and selling collateral and processes.

As the members of my Program will attest, the Six Pillars are represented in everything we give you on brand, marketing and selling inside my program, by way of marketing copy, models, images and more.

Every time I tell you what we're doing inside my program, I'm telling you what you need to do if you are not joining my program okay?

To Summarise.

I've given you some good headlines and some good detail on the foundation part of the BluePrint but remember you need to combine this book with my first book.

Create your bookkeeping practice Playbook as a plan, which includes everything in the BluePrint and your napkin numbers. Then set about building your brand foundations, making sure to use the Six Pillars of Persuasion. There's a lot to take on board, but the good news is, we've proven time and time again that it's worth it.

Now let's move on to Products and Pricing.

Chapter 4 - Products and Pricing

If this is a tough subject for you, you're not alone. I'll start with the cold, hard fact that nine out of ten bookkeepers get products and pricing very wrong. And yes, early on in my business I was one of them. It took me nearly five years to nail it, and since then I've refined and improved our strategies and systems around pricing and products.

In my first book, *The Strategic Bookkeeper*, I give you information and exercises inside one of the playbooks (aka workbooks) to build out your products. More importantly, I explain why you need to use a fixed-price "outcome billing" model rather than charge hourly.

If you decide to join my program, you will gain access to the pricing academy, where you get templates, tools and coaching support to guarantee your success around products and pricing. It is also available to buy as a stand-alone outside of the program and you can see more information on that here https://www.thestrategicbookkeeper.global/pricingacademy.

My Experience.

To explain what you need to learn and build and implement around products and pricing, I'll tell you about my experience and give you an insight into what we do inside the Pricing Academy so you can recreate it all in your practice.

In 2015, I doubled my net profit by getting products and pricing right - that is, I developed my perfect version 1, fixed pricing model, which has come a long way since then and evolved into "outcome billing". Products and Pricing have become a cornerstone of how I maintain a profitable practice with raving fan clients and lots of joy and it's how you will too.

It's very common for my tribe to have a similar experience and double their profits when working with me on products and pricing. And actually, when I chatted to seven tribe members "live" on a success panel, a few of them talked about the impact of products, pricing and more, in a way I think will be really helpful to you - that's episode 88.

In my first five years in practice, I really f**ked up around pricing. Right now, I want to share my mistakes, relating them precisely to the BluePrint (so you can really focus on it as that diagnostics tool and checklist).

- Complex, bespoke products: I served up services tailored to each client's needs. I asked my prospects what they wanted and attached a fee to it. Which was me creating a new service offering every time – a time-sucking nightmare that bundles up the real bookkeeping with the other "stuff" like admin and accounts
- Broken pricing strategy: I charged hourly which is not a pricing strategy at all and even when I was charging "the right rate", hourly billing set me up to fail around the three key elements of my practice being 1) build a thriving practice 2) delight my clients 3) my dream on my terms - hourly billing fails on all 3
- Lack of Systemised Advisory and selling it: I had no idea that I could – and should – be offering a range of advisory services that would actually help my clients get more from the bookkeeping I was doing for them

And almost every bookkeeper I've met since then is making the same or similar mistakes.

Are you making these mistakes? Let me tell you something. Right now I'm sitting here, at my desk, 7.20am on a Friday morning, coffee in hand and I'm reading what I just told you and I'm thinking back to the early days when I was doing it wrong.

Back then, I was excited and I was naive.

If I read that, I would be thinking, "but why is that wrong? All that seems logical".

And I get it. It does. If you're in an "employee mindset" just like I was. My goodness, "employee mindset" took me 13 years to name - you can listen to that subject at episode 2 of my podcast.

You are not an employee anymore. You are a business owner. You need to think and act like one. You need a systemised business, and that includes pricing.

Lessons from the Tribe

It was the most incredible thing to me, recently when members of my tribe (publicly during the success panel) told me that before they joined my program, they weren't running their businesses; their business and their clients were running them. They told me that now, 12 months in, one of the most impactful things is that they now have a real business.

To you I want to say... Trust me now, believe me later. You don't need to 100% understand everything including the nuances of pricing to lean in, learn and implement ok.

You can benefit from my experience, follow my proven systems and let the magic happen.

Benefiting from my mistakes

As you can now probably see from both my books, in terms of "mistakes", boy, have I been there done that. Costly, costly mistakes in virtually every part of my practice. Mistakes you can learn from and either stop making or avoid. How good is that!

Unfortunately, nine out of ten bookkeepers won't ever figure it out to a point where the effort makes it all worthwhile. You'll hear some of these bookkeepers tell you, "Oh I'm so busy" but beware the busy bookkeeper my friend; busy does not always mean thriving.

I was busy in my first five f**k up years too and if you had asked, "Jeannie, how's it all going" I would have said, "I'm busy".

What assumption do you make when a Bookkeeper says "I'm busy"? It's usually that they're successful. Another learning to take away from this book - Busy does not always mean thriving.

In fact, when my practice was finally, truly thriving I wasn't busy at all, I was enjoying all the time-wealth I had created from it.

You'll hear me repeat the nine out of ten statistic a few times throughout this book and with good reason because, unfortunately,

Nine out of ten bookkeepers also believe they won't be the nine out of ten

They're stuck in the "logical but broken systems that will keep them stuck", and that's why I want to harp on about it a bit, okay?

I really want you to step out from all this and succeed.

Learning from my mistakes, becoming one of the 10% who build a good solid practice with income and time-wealth.

Benefiting from the BluePrint

It's from my years of experience that I created this BluePrint.

I needed to build the BluePrint because I never want to forget where I was or how I got here.

Seeing how the BluePrint works in my program, and being able to compare myself and my results to those of my tribe has really helped me understand all over again, the impact of products and pricing.

What you need to do.

Before we dive into how to build and implement your products and pricing strategy, I just want to remind you how important it is to...

1. Plan for success
2. Get your mindset right
3. Set yourself up to be highly productive
4. Have your brand foundations in place
5. Have an on-point conversion process

In other words, you're going to need to nail everything on that left-hand side of the

BluePrint to ensure that products and pricing work as well as possible.

Why? Because your smart strategic products and pricing system is a piece of the success-puzzle right? But it works in conjunction with everything else on the BluePrint, and that's very important to remember.

I would love to have you join us inside my program because we nail that left-hand side *for you and with you*. In real-world terms, this is within 14 days of joining. You can actually do all these in a day inside the program, but I like to say 14 days to be conservative. Plus, that's what I see in the program, 14 days if you embrace progress over perfection.

So, if all this ever gets too hard, remember the tribe and I are there for you, ok.

Ok, look at your BluePrint and let's do this!

If you look at the BluePrint now, there are three parts to product and pricing, which are:

1. Smart, Simple Suite of Products
2. Robust Pricing Strategy
3. Incorporating Advisory

While writing this chapter, I actually used what I'm teaching you here to record a 4 part series of podcasts, which I'd love to point you to now - episodes 75 to 77, which starts with "plan for success" and moves onto 3 episodes called "pricing for profit and joy".

Honestly, what I share in those episodes... let's just say I wish I had that kind of support in the early years of running my practice.

My podcast is easy to find under "The Strategic Bookkeeper" or you can visit https://www.thestrategicbookkeeper.global/the-strategic-bookkeeper-podcast.

Step One: Develop a smart, simple suite of products.

First, let's take a moment to break down what a 'product' actually means when we're talking about bookkeeping services.

I could easily dedicate an entire book to productising your bookkeeping service—and in fact, I've already done several podcasts on this topic. But there is one in particular, I created while writing this chapter, which breaks down what productising is, why it's important and how to do it and that is episode 91.

If you want, you can even pause reading, check out the podcast, and come back once you've soaked it all in.

Before we move on, though, let me give you one more example that goes beyond what's in the podcast—a real-world look at productisation. For this, I'll use your local gym as an example.

Let's say you join a gym to use their equipment. You might even hire a personal trainer to create a program for you—that's a service. Whether you realise it or not, three factors drive your decision to buy any service: relationship, convenience, and price. In this case, you're likely going to the gym because of convenience and price.

And that's exactly what happens to many bookkeepers. Without knowing it, their clients are staying for convenience and price, which is a shakeable, breakable bookkeeping practice.

Now, imagine the gym up the road invites you in to check out their facility. Convenience and price are exactly the same as your current gym, but this one knows how to productise their service. They show you their ten-point plan to get you from where you are now to where you want to be.

Which looks something like this:

1. A consultation to understand why you've come to the gym and to review any specific medical conditions (ie: diabetes) and also goals like weight loss, muscle gain and so on
2. A review of your current lifestyle and your mind, body, spirit - to understand how you're eating, sleeping, moving and feeling (because stress levels and emotions play a role too)
3. A body scan to take a snapshot of your current body composition
4. A report that's wraps this all up into a NOW analysis
5. A personalised plan to work around your lifestyle that details how to eat, move and sleep
6. A vault of remarkable resources like courses, resources and other vetted professionals who you might need to help you on your journey

7. Options that allow you to work out at the gym and also at home or while you're travelling, to lower barriers to achieving your goals
8. A private community, the other members of the gym plus team HQ - who come together to support one another, and so you can ask questions and get support any day, anytime, anywhere
9. Weekly check-ins to ask if you're on track or off track and offer support
10. Quarterly diagnostics consultations to review your progress and modify your plan

Same facilities, price, and convenience—but the latter gym knows that the real value of their gym lies not in the gym itself but in their ability to help their members to get the outcome they want. Which one sounds more appealing?

The latter, of course.

Sell like a travel agent

Learning to sell the outcome is like learning to sell a beautiful holiday destination rather than the long-haul flight to get there. Imagine you've booked a holiday to Paris, one you've been dreaming of for quite some time. You are telling all your friends about your upcoming trip, in detail, not about the long-haul flight to get there, that's just a necessary evil, but still, one that you've paid a lot of money for.

Just because you've paid for the long-haul flight doesn't mean you value it. Just because you paid for the gym membership and the treadmills and the weights you lift doesn't mean that's what you value, that's the necessary evil to help you lose weight, look good, improve your energy levels, live longer and so on.

The same applies to your bookkeeping service, which is, unfortunately, like a long-haul flight. Productise it and you'll start selling the more appealing and valuable outcome aka destination. Get it?

To reiterate, because this is important my friend...

Just because we fork out a lot of money for something doesn't make it valuable ie: long haul flight, speeding fine, bookkeeping!

But don't worry, I promise as you read on I'll continue to show you how to productise bookkeeping and sell the outcome to make it so valuable, your clients can't imagine life without you.

Once upon a time, I was sitting in a villa in Ubud Bali when a prospective client called with a catch up job for me. Long story short, to illustrate the power of selling the outcome, ultimately, I said to this Prospect, "give me your credit card, and I'll give you a good night's sleep" to which he replied, "how did you know?"

I'll never forget that because it was a time when I was depending on my understanding of this stuff, of my value being in things like "a good night's sleep" rather than the bookkeeping - game changing for my practice.

Me taking over the bookkeeping was just the long-haul flight he needed to take to get to destination, "peace of mind, good night's sleep" which is why my focus was on that and why he was quite happy to press go in an instant, even if my price-tag was double my competitors.

My competitors were selling bookkeeping, I was selling peace of mind. Remember the V-Bar story? Same product, different pitch!

Productising and selling outcomes rather than hours will give you a massive competitive edge (just like in the gym example). It took me a while, but I nailed it and that's exactly what we facilitate inside my signature program too.

Now that you understand more about productising your service, let's dive into what a smart, simple suite of products looks like, why you need them, and how to implement them.

Remember I mentioned one of the mistakes I made early on was asking my prospective clients what they needed and then creating the service based on what they said? This usually ended up bundling the bookkeeping (aka double-entry accounting) with any admin and accounts work they needed and then attaching a fee.

That was a recipe for a time-sucking, inefficient nightmare called "tailored services." Not scalable.

What you need is a smart, simple suite of products which looks like this:

1. **A File Health Check Productised Service.** By now, you've read my first book, so you know this is the key entry point—the first thing you'll sell to prospective clients. This makes them ten times more likely to buy the next service from you, which is...

2. **Catch-Up/Rectification Productised Service.** Most of the time, everyone needs one of these. This work is impossible to scope. It took me a decade to nail a perfect productised service that converts incredibly well even though I charge more than most. This one, beautiful template serves 100% of my clients with the occasional modification. After all the catch-up/rectification pain is cleared up, then we move onto proposing either full service or DIY support...

3. **Full Service Strategic Bookkeeping Productised Service.** We have developed the most perfect template which suits everyone who needs full-service bookkeeping. First and foremost, it includes outcome-centric features like courses and resources to support our clients in optimising their business performance. Plus, all the features and functions of the double-entry accounting, compliance and support. Importantly, there is no admin, accounts or other ad hoc work in this template because that stuff can't be templated very easily.

4. **A DIY Bookkeeper Support Productised Service.** Some clients will be suited to doing the day to day themselves and so,

we have a fabulous template for them. It's very similar to the one previous except of course, they're electing to do the day to day. This template includes clauses about our expectations and what we'll do if we find they get it wrong.

5. **Add-On Out-of-Scope Services.** Remember that admin and accounts and other ad hoc work? This is where we create it - we have some templates, based on what we've done for other clients but on the whole, we simply write up the bits and bobs we're agreeing to here ie: stripe downloads, checking admin email, logging into banking portals and so on. Aim for the 80/20 principle where 80% is templated for same/same work and 20% is written up to product stack in your proposal

6. **Full service OR Payroll Support Productised Service.** If our clients have a payroll they choose from one of these two. They don't get to opt out, payroll is too easy to stuff up and so, it's either or here. Both are very similar it's just with the full service one, we're doing the weekly or fortnightly payroll processing as well as the other "heavy lifting" as we like to call it

We have others and you will too. Others like:

1. Strategic Bookkeeping/Investigate the Numbers
2. Software set up
3. Software Training
4. Systems Analysis, recruitment and other advisory services
5. Business Coaching Packages

And so on. The key is to separate the real bookkeeping from admin and accounts, create templates and product-stack into your proposals to make it all efficient and scalable.

Ahhhh efficient and scalable, how good does that sound? Yes!

As you'll discover in Step Two, when we dive into robust pricing strategy, you should only ever bill monthly (never quarterly), and make sure you adhere to your minimum one-off and monthly job charges.

Lessons from the Tribe

More than 80% of the bookkeepers who join my program do not have this dialed in. They use the Pricing Academy to do that. And 100% of them tell me it's like the heavens opening, transformational.

We use Ignition

We use Ignition software as our practice management tool to engage clients in our productised services. With Ignition, we can product stack, for example, full-service bookkeeping plus payroll support plus monthly advisory meetings. We can also quickly and easily create out-of-scope admin and accounts products, then use them as templates for similar work when needed.

Ignition has been one of the best decisions I've made in my bookkeeping practice. It's saved me a lot of time and money, and it's definitely a piece of tech that acts like an extra team member. My tribe rave about Ignition too.

If you're not using Ignition, you should be.

At the back of this book, I've provided details on how to get in touch with Ignition, along with a special offer they've made available to my readers. Enjoy!

Lessons from the tribe on Ignition.

Many of our tribe subscribe to Ignition software and I thought it would be helpful to interview one of them and so, you can listen to me interview Emily Sinderberry at episode 95.

We use Dext.

I touched on Dext a bit in my first book, but I want to emphasise that, like Ignition, we simply couldn't operate at this level without the Dext suite in our bookkeeping practice. Without Dext, our efficiency would plummet, costs would skyrocket, and we'd lose that all-important joy and peace of mind.

Why? Well, it's an inversion situation (classic bookkeeper talk, right?). The Dext products reduce keystrokes, minimise errors, lessen our dependency on additional staff, elevate the client experience, and save us massive amounts of time and money.

We use Dext Prepare—a fantastic tool to manage bills and receipts, and it continues to impress us with new features that keep getting better. Then, there's Dext Precision, which I want to highlight in relation to your file health checks and catch-up rectification work.

When we first started with Dext Precision, I loved using the file health score. I could bring on a new client and get a quick snapshot by running their file through Precision—it's like an instant health check.

Now, Precision's file health feature is just one of its many strengths. Precision has genuinely revolutionised our practice. In this chapter, I really wanted to demonstrate to you how we use it in the file health check and catch-up rectification processes - so you can follow suit.

I have a few podcasts you can listen to, to find out why I can't live without Dext - A recent interview with a tribe member on how she uses Dext is Episode 96 and, my interview with the CEO (that had my jaw drop) is episode 90.

Productised Services Inside the Pricing Academy

Inside the academy, we give you a folder of templates you can use. Those templates include everything I've discussed here—and then some.

It's basically my first 13 years in practice, with all my templates refined and ready to go.

If you have any questions, feel free to shoot me an email.

Lessons from the Tribe on Pricing

Here's a quote from Karen, a member of our program:

"When I joined Jeannie's program and got her pricing calculator, the ability to calculate the price based on transaction volume (all built into the calculator) was so helpful. Applying this to my practice meant I could streamline and save time and money."

Now that you understand how to productise and what it looks like to create a smart, simple suite of products, let's move on to **robust pricing strategy**.

Step Two: Robust Pricing Strategy

By now, I know you've read my first book and digested everything on products and pricing. And again, I'll refer you to episodes 74 to 77 on planning and pricing. They're worth listening to before reading on if you haven't already.

Your robust pricing strategy has a few key pillars:

- Outcome Billing
- Minimum One-Off Job Charge
- Minimum Monthly Job Charge

And some absolute no-no's:

- No hourly billing
- No quarterly work

If you paused to listen to those podcast episodes, what I share next will be a little rinsing and repeating, which is always great for deepening your understanding and implementing these concepts.

Beyond what I shared in my first book on pricing, I think it would be helpful to share what I've learned from my tribe members. There are so many stories, but here are just a few.

Kate's story

Kate joined my program in August 2023 after 40 years as one of the most skilled bookkeepers I've ever met—plus an all-around wonderful human. She told me that my program was going to be her last-ditch attempt at making her bookkeeping practice work.

By January, within just five months, Kate's practice was well and truly coming along. Within 12 months, she had recruited her first full-time staff member and more than tripled her profits. A big part of this success was getting her products, pricing, and conversion processes right.

In fact, the program paid for itself through these parts alone, just like you see in the BluePrint.

Note: Kate's profit growth was 330% whereas her revenue was 270%. If your revenue is growing more than your profit, you have a broken model (like I did early on).

Kate cites confidence as the number one thing she gained from our program. Watching Kate go from fear, doubt and indecision to rock-star confidence will stay with me forever - this is why I do what I do.

The key takeaway here? Kate followed our products and pricing methodology to a 'T' - and it worked.

Anne

Anne had been a bookkeeper in practice for 20 years when she joined our program, taking over a bookkeeping practice full of clients and some legacy staff.

Before joining, Anne had already used what she learned from my podcast to move from hourly to fixed-price billing. This gave her consistency and increased her client satisfaction—exactly what it's supposed to do.

But when Anne joined our program, we discovered she was charging about 40% less than she needed to make it worthwhile (a common tale). Since she had just moved to fixed pricing, she decided to go step-by-step, implementing everything in the BluePrint over the next year while carefully doubling her rates for all her clients.

Anne says that having the brand foundations in place, along with everything else on the left-hand side of the BluePrint, allowed her to double her fees while only losing a couple of clients - because what you implement from that left-hand side of the BluePrint connects your clients to your value rather than the price.

Paris rather than the long-haul flight – remember?

Anne's results were just shy of 6 figures. Anne has now become a bit of an expert in products and pricing, supporting her fellow tribe members inside our Mastermind community (our private Facebook group).

I encourage Anne to get involved in our coaching and implementation sessions whenever products and pricing come up.

Verity

When Verity joined our program, she was living off her savings. A year later, she was at six figures, had a 12-week waiting list, and was recruiting her first full-time all-rounder to take on more of that wait-list work.

Verity describes the done-for-you collateral in the program as "mind-blowing" and says she's been able to convert 90% of her inquiries into the *products* I've demonstrated here - high value, high price tag, raving fan clients.

The income is there and increasing, and the time wealth will follow. I'm so excited for Verity.

Minimum Job Charges - A Game Changer

Most of what you need to know about outcome billing is in my first book and the many podcasts I've shared with you. Right now, I want to expand just a little bit on minimum job charges—starting with the **Minimum One-Off Job Charge**.

It is quite simple (remembering that simple doesn't necessarily mean easy).

For one-off work, in 2024, my practice has a minimum one-off job charge of $1,300. For example, if you need me for a job that'll take 15 minutes, that's $1,300. If you need me for a job that'll take three hours, that's still $1,300.

I'm not selling hours—I'm selling outcomes. And my clients are raving fans who enjoy the destinations I take them to.

And, I'm putting myself first. What I mean by that is that I'm focusing on making sure I build a rock-solid, viable bookkeeping practice before trying to help my clients. I won't be able to help anyone if I build a broken business with no time and no money to support anyone.

Make no mistake that profit and cash are like oxygen for a business, and your practice is no exception. If you build a broken business without enough profit and cash, it'll suffocate and eventually it'll die.

As a woman and a mother, for the longest time, I thought my job was to put everyone else first. I talk about this in my first book. As women and mothers, this is something we tend to transfer into our business world.

Can I tell you something I learned the hard way? You need to put yourself first—in business and life. Only when you do that will you have the health—mentally, physically, spiritually, and financially—to take care of anyone else.

What's your minimum one-off job charge?

If I knocked on your door tomorrow and had a 15-minute job for you, what would you quote me?

My recommendation

If you want to keep it simple, just do what I do. Otherwise, in 2024, I recommend your minimum one-off job charge be at least $600, whether that's USD, CAD, AUD, GBP, NZD, etc - that rate will work as a BAM (Bare Ass Minimum).

For example: if you're going to train someone in the basics of using Intuit or Xero etc, package it up as "up to 3 hours over recorded zoom, plus 3 months support on the subjects covered" for $595 plus tax.

For that package, I'd charge $1295, and actually, I have that wrapped up as an amazing productised service for software training that my tribe and I use, and our clients love it.

Now onto **Minimum Monthly Job Charge,**

In 2024 ours is about $270 per month, regardless of how long the job takes.

For the same reasons as the minimum one-off job charge. Simple right?

You might be wondering why the minimum monthly charge is so much lower than the one-off charge. Here's why: You get to benefit from my 15 years of experience, having made all the mistakes, having figured it all out, having built the income and lifestyle I wanted within five or six years, and having refined everything so I could confidently coach you. That's why (wink).

But, to expand a little...

Once a client has gone through the customer experience—buying a file health check, catch-up work, and now committing to me long-term, making them a VIP.

I can look at that value of that job many ways:

- Annual value
- Lifetime value
- Raving fan referring VIP client

While the one-off job had a value of $1300 and a profit margin of say, $1100, my VIP has

- An annual value of $3,240 with a profit margin of say, $2,600 or so
- A lifetime profit-value of between $26,000 and, well the sky is the limit, but based on experience, $150,000 (as they tend to upgrade into advisory)
- Plus, the value of the word-of-mouth marketing that will come from them as well

This minimum job charge commonly comes into its own for productised services like a simple DIY bookkeeping job. Traditionally, this might have been a quarterly job, which you now know is a big no-no.

Once again, you can't help anyone if you have a broken business model. What I'm showing you here is exactly what you need to learn and do to build a viable bookkeeping practice that not only survives but thrives—and that's the only way you'll help anyone.

Now, let's say a prospective client knocked on your door today and told you they just need you to check their file and lodge their compliance quarterly. What would you charge them? Would it be $3,240 a year?

Come on, be honest with yourself. The courage to be open, honest, and vulnerable is a cornerstone of success. The opportunity right now is to look at what you're doing versus what you *need* to be doing—and change direction.

That's right. You're at a fork in the road, and what I want for you right now is to head towards this destination: *a thriving practice, delighted clients, and your dream on your terms*. Rather than destination "busy" but not thriving.

Before we dive into **Step 3: Incorporating Advisory**, let's take a moment to talk about using a **Pricing Calculator**.

Quite simply—you need one. I covered this in my first book, and right now, I think it would be helpful to share a story and what the Tribe has to say about our pricing calculator.

Lisa's Story

When Lisa joined my program in 2024, she was 4 years into owning and operating her own bookkeeping practice, with two staff members assisting her. Lisa had tried another well-known bookkeeping coach and did not get the return on investment to make it worthwhile. Once bitten, twice shy. Fortunately, Lisa took the leap of faith to join us, and 6 months in, she was rocking it - full up with a waitlist, recruiting her next full-time staff member.

Lisa says, "The pricing calculator is fantastic. Upon joining, I was able to use it to see what I needed to do with my legacy clients, as well as how to calculate fees for new clients. The calculator allowed me to increase my profits quickly and contributed to paying for the program quickly, too. I use the pricing calculator to repackage clients when our traffic light system (also included in the program) tells me too. Such an impactful tool."

I love seeing Lisa in our implementation sessions. Showing up. Doing it. I just love it.

Sadly, many bookkeepers won't join us because they've been burnt by another coach. They'll stay held back by baggage from a relationship that went wrong. I hope that's not you.

Do you have a pricing calculator?

If you don't, you need to build one—or gain access to ours by joining either our Pricing Academy or The Transformation Program.

Step 3 Incorporating Advisory

As you can see on the BluePrint, part of products and pricing is selling advisory from the get-go. In this example, where we have a minimum monthly job charge for a DIY bookkeeping support package, we likely would have recommended something like **Level One Advisory**, which is **Strategic Bookkeeping**—investigating the numbers. That would have brought the total annual value of that client to $6,240.

So, once again, compare what you're doing now to what you need to be doing to build a rock-solid, viable bookkeeping practice—one with raving fan clients, and ultimately, the income and lifestyle you want and deserve.

Write it down. Your now, your future. And may I suggest, if you're reading this book, your future is here. Well done.

In the interest of saving you time, I'll point you to my first book and the chapter "Succession" as your "how to" guide on advisory.

See you in the next chapter!

Chapter 5 - Product Ladder

In my first book I introduced you to the product ladder, and I went into it in some detail.

That said, I'll give you a quick refresher in this chapter. But if you're a bookkeeper, whether already in practice or just starting, and you want to be part of the 10% who succeed—building a thriving practice with delighted clients, generating the income and lifestyle you initially aimed for—then you will do the work. You'll give me the hours, the attitude and no excuses. So, if you haven't yet, go back and read my first book, okay?

If you take a look at the BluePrint, you'll notice that the product ladder is on the left-hand side. It contains four key parts:

1. **Content** – Think website, social media, etc.
2. **Welcome** – Gated nurture assets.
3. **Core** – Your core services - productised.
4. **Succession** – Which means what's next? Which is your advisory suite.

Beyond what you've already learned in my first book, in this chapter, I'll help you understand *why* the product ladder is such an essential part of the Bookkeeping Practice BluePrint. Specifically, why it's on the left-hand side and why I recommend you nail this before you even answer the door to a prospective client.

Here's the magic of a smart, strategic product ladder:

- Properly constructed, it gives your market a place to get to know, like and trust you 24/7 online (**content/welcome**)
- It engages your market, warming them up to buy from you and it does that with less of the traditional hustle and effort, which is very important (**welcome lines**).
- Once warmed up by your product ladder, you will, more easily, convert prospects into paying clients, particularly given the first thing you'll charge money for is a file health check (welcome line)
- Your product ladder will improve the conversion rates of all your products - as a rule, this means that for the same or less effort, you'll make more money - that's working smarter rather than harder

- You'll find you'll be able to onboard clients without price as a priority - a well-constructed product ladder and customer experience will keep your clients connected to the destination rather than the long haul flight - in the transformation program, part of that is your signature brochure and video sales letter
- Your product ladder will upgrade your clients into more advisory services which is really the golden ticket in terms of scaling your profits and your client satisfaction

In fact, you'll find that while the ongoing monthly services is ultimately the highest ticket product your client buys, it will be the easiest sale you'll make in the process due to the strategy behind the Product Ladder (and the power of the BluePrint as a whole).

In the program, I like to say, "the $99 file health check is the hardest sale you'll ever make, and the $20,000 ongoing services is the easiest sale" - that's just how human psychology (and persuasion) works and why it's so important to install a well-constructed product ladder into your practice. Otherwise, you'll miss the opportunity and you'll miss out on helping more clients.

Consistently climbing your Product Ladder

Remember the **Six Pillars of Persuasion** we covered earlier? Your product ladder incorporates nearly all of them. But I want to draw your attention to one in particular - **consistency**.

As you deepen your understanding of the product ladder, I want you to notice how the pillar of consistency works. Humans are hardwired to act consistently. In terms of the product ladder, this means that your market is more likely to keep taking steps up the ladder, consistently. That's why the last conversion—the one with the highest price tag—ends up being the easiest. It's the pillar of consistency at work.

This is one of the ways our tribe achieves such high conversion rates, from inquiry to VIP, using the power of the product ladder and the pillar of persuasion: consistency.

Lessons from The Tribe

Elsie had only been in practice for six months when she joined my program. Twelve months later, she told me her conversion rate had hit 90%, even though she was charging significantly higher rates than her competitors. You don't get those kinds of conversion rates without a solid product ladder.

Belinda, another member, joined the program five years into her practice. Her business was already profitable, and she was getting a lot of things right, including her product and pricing fundamentals. But she told me that implementing the product ladder paid for the program within 8 weeks. She hadn't been charging for the file health check, and she was charging less than us for catch-up and rectification work.

She began charging more and converting more clients at higher rates. She's now looking forward to converting existing clients (VIP's) into advisory using what we give her in the program, which she'll have her team deliver because, training your team in how to deliver advisory is included in our program.

No matter where you are on your bookkeeping journey, a product ladder is essential to maximise the opportunities that exist when a prospective client knocks on your door.

Think of your practice like an orange. We want to squeeze every last ounce of juice from it. That's what Belinda did—she took a good practice and made it better. There's always room for improvement right?

The Absence of a Product Ladder

When you fail to build a smart, strategic product ladder, you'll convert far fewer prospective clients into VIPs. You'll lose work to competitors and find yourself competing on price. This means you'll be working hard, not smart.

That old chestnut about working smarter, not harder? It means doing the same (or less) work for a much bigger result—and that's what a product ladder will do for you.

Once again, the global statistic is that 9 out of 10 bookkeepers fail to find the success that makes it all worthwhile, and the absence of a product ladder plays a significant role in that failure.

Audit your Product Ladder

I recommend you do a bit of an audit of your product ladder. Once you do that, you'll be able to write down what you need to build and implement across the four parts of your product ladder.

And from there, you can decide whether to do it on your own or get it done for and with you inside our program.

As I sit here, I'm imagining you reading this. I want to snap my fingers and magically appear in front of you to say, "Join my program!" Why? Because I know the value of the product ladder I provide for you in the program, and I want to give you the best chance to succeed.

But, ultimately, it's a choose-your-own-adventure, and I'll do everything I can to help you through **The Strategic Bookkeeper Project,** which includes my books, podcast, starter membership, stand-alone courses and resources and my signature program.

Step One: Your Content

To refresh you on what I've already shared in my first book on content—step one on your product ladder—this is the information you share freely at no cost to show your market who you are and how you can solve their problems.

Remember, you're in the problem-solving game.

If you're anything like me, it's easy to undervalue your content. You might think of it as the basic marketing stuff we have put on our website and social media. But content is valuable! Anything you put out there to show people who you are and the specific problems you solve is incredibly helpful.

And it's the first thing prospects need to know about you, so no wonder it's step one on your product ladder.

Think of your own behaviour as a consumer. You tend to start with a "Google search", right? You look at general information about the products or services you're after. That's content.

When it comes to website content, nobody does it better than **Bizink**. Less than 10% of bookkeeper websites hit the mark. Which means 90% of bookkeeper websites miss the mark. That's interesting, given that 90% of bookkeepers are failing to earn more than they could in a decent job.

If you join my program, **Bizink** has a website template that includes our done-for-you product ladder and our other licensed materials. Whether you join or not, you're welcome to reach out to **Bizink**—there's a special offer for readers at the back of this book.

Step Two: Welcome Line Nurture Assets

Is this my favourite part of the product ladder? Probably.

Why? Well, I'm obsessed with pipelines. I love helping my tribe create a visible and invisible pipeline of prospective clients who've already spent time getting to know, like, and trust them through their product ladder, warmed up, and ready to buy, irrespective of price.

Step one (content) and step two (welcome) work together to build that pipeline. But step two - these welcome line nurture assets - is what really nurtures your audience through the customer journey until they knock on your door and/or refer you to others (advocacy, which you learnt about in my first book). This is where the real magic happens, in my opinion.

Welcome line nurture assets are gated. That "gate" is simply a form that requires contact details. These assets engage your audience, prompting them to tell you, "Houston, I have a problem."

In the chapter on audience building and nurturing, we'll dive deeper into this.

It took me a long time and plenty of failures to develop the welcome line nurture assets we have today in the Transformation Program. Since opening the doors to my program, I've learned a lot from working with my tribe. Watching them use their product ladders to find, onboard, and retain clients - without price being the priority - brings me so much joy. And as a bonus, I get to refine my processes as we go. Meanwhile, my program members are getting booked solid and even starting waiting lists.

Here are the **10 welcome line nurture assets** I've refined over more than a decade that we give you in the Transformation Program.

1. Various forms of consultations, including needs analysis.
2. File Health Check.
3. Business Health Check.
4. Now/Future Analysis.

5. 20-Min Call Process.
6. Annual Planning Session.
7. 7 Deadly Sins eBook.
8. Better in Business Podcast.
9. Video Sales Letter.
10. Training Event.

These 10 welcome line nurture assets aren't in any particular linear order. They form an ecosystem of high-value gifts you can give to both your market and your clients. Remember the **pillar of persuasion, reciprocity**? Altogether, these gift assets provide a combination of:

- Education.
- Diagnostics.
- Planning.
- How-to instructions.
- Consultation and recommendations.

These nurture assets (gifts) move the needle in your prospective clients' (and clients') businesses—helping them do better in business even before buying from you. They build trust and credibility, which is essential to your PCs' willingness to part with their hard-earned cash and work with you.

Stories from the Tribe

Rachel joined our program after two years as a self-employed bookkeeper. She followed our program diligently and used the BluePrint, regularly sending her database the **Better in Business Podcast** on a fortnightly basis.

The **Better in Business Podcast** is from the www.betterinbusiness.global platform that I developed to serve Strategic Bookkeepers and their market - clients and PC's (prospective clients). The podcast educates entrepreneurs on how to do better in business and explains that Strategic Bookkeeping is Pillar one. It's like a little done-for-you lead generation.

One day, in an implementation session, Rachel shared a win with us all. A prospective client on her database, who had been dormant for a long time, emailed her after listening to a podcast, asking to catch up.

If you're in my tribe, you know that catch-up means a needs analysis, which Rachel conducted. During the needs analysis, she asked the most powerful question you can ask in this process: "Tell me about yourself."

Tom, the PC, poured his heart out about his struggles to do better in business. He said he'd been looking at his bank account to measure performance, which the podcast helped him realise was a big mistake. "I now know that only my books can do that," he told Rachel.

The podcast taught Tom that he needed to get his books up to date and then actually look at the numbers to see how his business was performing in order to make informed decisions. And for that, he needed a strategic bookkeeper, the one who'd been there all along, but until now, he didn't understand the value of.

Here is, point by point, the system that Rachel followed which is also represented in the chapters of this book and visually on the BluePrint. After the needs analysis she:

- Sold Tom a welcome line - File Health Check for $99
- Once done, she debriefed with Tom and sold him the catch-up job required, phase one was $1300
- As Tom required a bit more on that front, she sold him some more catch-up products for a grand total of $3300

- After that, Rachel made personal recommendations for monthly bookkeeping and advisory for $20,000 per annum, which, of course, Tom jumped at because from the get-go, Rachel and Tom were connected to the destination, to Paris - in this case, "doing better in business."

Not long after Rachel started working with Tom, they identified more problems Tom needed to solve, so Rachel proposed additional services—specifically, a systems analysis and a recruitment job to find a key administrator. These additional services totalled around $15,000.

The product ladder works for you and your clients.

Tom now has the education and support he needs from Rachel to build his dream business and life. He's a raving fan, getting a great return on his investment and singing Rachel's praises to everyone he knows. Recently, Tom referred his friend Rob for a consultation after hearing another **Better in Business Podcast** episode.

In the chapter on audience building, we'll elaborate more on this, as finding and engaging an audience go hand in hand. **Content** and **Welcome Line Nurture Assets** are how you engage your audience.

A Word on Consultations

I'll keep this fairly brief, but I want to give you some important information to steer you in the right direction and away from any misinformation you might have heard around consultations.

Has anyone ever suggested that you provide prospective clients with a free, one-hour consultation? Is that something you're currently doing or have thought about doing?

My advice is simple: your free consultation, which should be a **needs analysis**, should last between 5 and 15 minutes and be conducted over the phone. Fast, simple and highly effective.

The rule of thumb I work with is that anything beyond 15 minutes should be charged for. It took me a long time to figure this out in my own practice, and right now, you have the opportunity to benefit from my mistakes, my learning, and my refining.

Remember the chapter on **getting it done** and the section on **productivity**? Learning and implementing what I teach you about consultations will free up your time. And if you don't already know, your time will become your most valuable and coveted resource.

Lessons from the Tribe

Jane joined my program brand new to running her own bookkeeping practice. If you're a little further along in your journey, take a moment to think back to the beginning. Like me, you were probably excited and a little naive.

Jane was, too.

She told me she planned to conduct in-person consultations, which she would travel to, for free. From experience, I knew this was a mistake. We discussed it, but Jane assured me she had plenty of free time and felt this would be a great way to build relationships. Against my better judgment, I trusted Jane, and she went ahead.

Later, when I spoke to Jane, she had become incredibly busy with these free, in-person consultations and a range of other activities that kept her busy but not productive. These kinds of things are just like being a hamster on a wheel—you gain speed, you gain traction, but you're going nowhere.

Trust me now, believe me later: whether you have lots of time on your hands or none at all, *start as you mean to go on*. Follow the rules and play to win.

Do your consultations as a **needs analysis** over the phone in under 15 minutes, and then sell a **File Health Check** for $99. To get this right, you'll need to nail the conversion process outlined in my first book, or you're welcome to join my program to do this.

What if you find, during the consultation, that you need more than 15 minutes to understand your PC's needs?

Actually, you will need more than 15 minutes and you'll get that in the paid file health check and during the first piece of "project work" which is usually catch-up and rectification. You see these both form part of how you go deeper on what your client needs. Make sense?

Trust this process; it's a fork in the road. It's a key strategy you need to thrive.

In my experience and *lessons from the tribe*, this process fits almost every client every time.

Other forms of needs analysis

During this process, as you dive into your clients' file and their business with them, you'll naturally be doing lots of diagnostics, your brain will be ticking over as you gain a broader picture of their business strengths, weaknesses and so on. A lot like a doctor doing their diagnostics.

And just like a doctor, you might discover that more "tests" are necessary - especially for bigger businesses with staff, for example...

- A business review
- An accounts review
- A systems review
- A systems needs analysis
- A software needs analysis
- An SOP analysis (SOP means - standard operating procedures)

And so on. Great. At that point, you can have a conversation with your client (remember, they're no longer a prospect because they've spent at least $99 with you) about the need to analyse further.

In my experience, most entrepreneurs are thrilled to have finally found someone (you) with the skills and interest to help them find what's broken and fix it.

This is a big subject, and every bookkeeper will have a different breadth of knowledge on it, so we'll leave it there. I encourage you to use what I've shown you in real life because you learn by doing my friend. Progress over perfection ok.

If you'd like me to go deeper into this, send me an email and request a podcast on the subject.

Step Three: Core Products

Everyone has **core products**. Ultimately, these are what you sell once you've completed the initial **File Health Check** and **catch-up rectification work** that generally comes first.

You can read more about this in my first book.

Step Four: Succession Products

Succession means "next." What's next for your clients? As a rule, this will be your **advisory suite**. The chapter on succession in my first book gives you an incredible vault of information, along with templates to help you learn and implement advisory services.

It's worth mentioning again—when it comes to products and pricing, there's a massive opportunity to increase both your profit and your client's satisfaction by learning to sell advisory services from the get-go.

Lessons from the Tribe

Hearing feedback from my tribe members has been amazing, especially from those who have tried other advisory programs before. The problem with most of those programs is that they were built by accountants for accountants. While valuable, they don't tend to give bookkeepers the confidence they need to actually sell and deliver advisory services.

In contrast, my tribe tells me that the advisory module in our **Transformation Program** gives them exactly what they were looking for: the tools and the confidence to learn, implement, and involve their team in the advisory process.

My advisory system is designed by a bookkeeper for bookkeepers. It's simple, powerful, and has delivered six and seven-figure results for the bookkeepers' clients using the system all around the world.

Can you see why advisory services are a true investment while basic bookkeeping tends to be a cost? It's almost impossible to make real money through basic bookkeeping alone. But when you dig into the numbers with your clients—when you shine a light on how their business is really performing and ask the right questions—the magic happens. Your client gets the clarity and space to make smart, informed decisions.

It's simpler than you think! Many advisory programs make it unnecessarily complicated, but ours is beautifully simple to learn and deliver.

I'm also incredibly proud of the marketing and selling assets we provide around advisory. These are world-class and the first of their kind in the industry - one of the reasons the tribe will tell you that there is "no comparing The Transformation Program to any other coach or program".

Let's Summarise Your Product Ladder

Building a product ladder leverages the **Six Pillars of Persuasion**: it's an essential tool designed to guide your client through the customer journey—from problem to payoff. It helps them see and experience your value, removes price as a priority, and converts more lovely humans into clients you can truly help. And in turn, they help you build your rock-solid bookkeeping practice.

1. **Step One** is your brand foundation—**content**—which is not gated. Prospects don't have to give up anything to access it.
2. **Step Two** is your **Welcome Lines**, which are nurture assets designed to nurture your market through the customer journey to become a pipeline.
3. **Step Three** is your **Core Product**—your monthly packages.
4. **Step Four** is **Succession**—your advisory suite.

A word on Building and implementing your Product Ladder, specifically Welcome Line Nurture Assets

I know that the most efficient way to build and implement your product ladder is by joining my program. I know how long it took me to build, perfect and refine. And I know it works.

Your second option is to try it yourself and bring in professionals to help. If you choose this route, make sure you calculate the full cost of hiring those professionals and factor in the time for testing and refining everything until it works smoothly. I can tell you from experience this cost will likely be 10 times the investment in the **Transformation Program**. But often, it's only after you're deep down that rabbit hole—feeling frustrated—that you realise you wish you'd made a different choice.

I will tell you everything I possibly can to fast-track your success because I see too many bookkeepers hold themselves back for years, blaming time and money and bad experiences for inaction.

I priced my program at $99 USD per week to ensure I give my tribe members at least 10x the value. When you recruit us, you're effectively recruiting a $100k team.

Whichever path you choose, know that I'll be cheering you on.

The Conversion Process

We're moving through the BluePrint at a phenomenal rate, which is why I ask you to approach this methodically:

- Read **The Strategic Bookkeeper** first—twice.
- Read this book once for a general understanding.
- Then, go back and read it again, working through each concept, idea, and strategy.

Now, look at where we are on the BluePrint— at the **Conversion Process**. Some of you are already nodding your heads because you know what I'm about to say: I've already covered the **Conversion Process** comprehensively in **The Strategic Bookkeeper**, so you need to be familiar with that before you go any further.

The good news is much of what I've said here, particularly in regard to the **Product Ladder**, the **customer journey** via **Welcome Line Nurture Assets**, and **consultations**, is also in my first book.

How are we doing?

It's time to move on to the right-hand side of **The Bookkeeping Practice BluePrint**, but before we do, let's do a quick check-in. Let's review what we've covered so far.

- **Foundation**: Build a solid foundation with planning, mindset, productivity and brand foundations.
- **Financial Management**: Stay on top of your financial management, especially when it comes to hiring and managing a winning team.
- **Products and Pricing**: Create a smart, simple suite of products with a robust pricing strategy that includes advisory services.
- **Product Ladder**: This is your essential marketing tool, incorporating the Six Pillars of Persuasion to create a pipeline and drive high conversion rates.
- **Conversion Process**: Refer to my first book and the chapter on conversions for more on how to master this.

Before we move on, can you do me a favour? Can you promise me that once I teach you how to **find and engage an audience** (in the next chapter) which will ultimately become a pipeline, promise me you will use what I've taught you about the left-hand side of the BluePrint to turn prospects into - *your thriving* *practice with delighted clients and your dream on your terms.*

In one direction is a busy practice; you don't want that.

In the other direction is a thriving practice; this is what you want my friend.

So right now, before we move on, I'd like you to take a moment to print the BluePrint out and make the commitment to yourself and to me that you'll put in the hours and the attitude to learn and build, progress over perfection, to be one of the 10% of bookkeepers who get this stuff right.

Build thriving, my friend, not busy.

Engaged audience - here we come!

Chapter 6 - Finding and Engaging Your Audience.

In my first book, I wrote a chapter called The Power of Attraction, which breaks down how to find and engage your audience. It covers essentials like profile, results-based marketing, building databases, networking, winning clients, leveraging social media, crafting compelling messages, using the 'value' approach, and harnessing the power of advocacy.

I hope you've already read it not just once but twice, but if you haven't, skip off and do it now, and then come back.

Here, we'll continue with client attraction but from a new angle. Just as you're sharpening your skills with this book, I'm constantly levelling up by learning from the best—mentors and coaching programs that keep me at the top of my game. I don't just talk the talk—I walk it.

One mentor I really tune into is Claire Pelletreau, who talks extensively about finding and engaging audiences. Listening to Claire helped me frame my own approach to client attraction in a new way, which is - finding and engaging an audience.

Before we go any further, I'd like to begin with the end in mind - this is what I'd like you to do with what you learn from this chapter. So, here is a checklist of what you're going to learn and what you need to do, point by point, which I'll repeat at the end of the chapter. Let's call it your 10-point plan...

1. Focus on the first three audience-building strategies.
2. Remembering to nail the BluePrint with proven results before trying the last 2.
3. Every one of the audience-building strategies is an inch wide and a mile deep - you can work these forever, and they will build you a 6 or 7-figure thriving practice when combined with nailing the BluePrint.
4. Therefore, on these three strategies, keep asking yourself... what else, what else, what else?
5. Create a business development spreadsheet to use to work on these strategies.

6. Put your database in there so you can categorise and see them visually - that way, you'll connect with your database more deeply, human to human and be more likely to keep in touch with them in a relevant, authentic way.
7. Do also use a CRM like Mailchimp or https://www.officiently.com.au/ to do your strategic, keep-in-touch marketing.
8. Reserve time each morning to work on activities related to building and engaging your audience - new and existing.
9. Once you find an audience, get them onto your database and then nurture them with your product ladder.
10. Do both passive and active activities - active being the business development hat.

Strategies for Finding an Audience

If you look at the Bookkeeping Practice BluePrint, you'll see these five key audience attraction strategies, which we'll dive into in this chapter.

1. Existing Audience
2. Networking
3. EAP (Everygreen Advocacy Partnerships) - aka Partnership Marketing

4. Paid (primarily meta-ads - aka FB and Insta Ads)
5. Summits (a little like online conferences)

The first three on the list are the strategies I am going to get you to focus on first. The last two, which are paid and Summits, should only be used a) when you have got your entire BluePrint down pat and b) with the support of a professional like myself.

There are many more strategies you can use to find an audience; however, these are the ones that work the best and give you the best bang for your time and money, buck.

I want you to think of the first three on the list as *an inch wide and a mile deep*. These three audience attraction strategies, when combined with engagement and the rest of the BluePrint, will allow you to find all the clients you want and need.

Lessons from the tribe

A great example of this is Karen, a Tribe member I have featured on our podcast, in our success panel and earlier on in this book.

You may remember that when Karen joined us, she already had a successful bookkeeping practice. When interviewing Karen, she told me that after digesting all of my content, she realised she had built her practice on the power of the EAP - Evergreen Advocacy Partnerships (aka, partnership marketing).

Specifically, early on in her practice, Karen engaged a couple of ideal clients and as it happened, both of them served Karen"s ideal clients too. Karen managed to (for want of a better phrase) tap their databases by getting them to refer their clients to her.

Prior to joining my program, Karen was unaware of just how powerful this strategy was and how it had worked for her. It is so critically important to understand any success we have so that we can zoom in on it and get more out of that same strategy.

Plus, if you don't know how you got there, you may end up lost eventually - that's a breakable, shakeable business, my friend.

Karen built a practice with 10 staff because EAP and the others are *an inch wide but a mile deep*.

Lessons From The Tribe

Remember the law of polarity related to productivity in the chapter on getting it done?

Something I work very hard on in my program, rinsing and repeating every week, is encouraging my tribe not to go rogue on me, particularly when it comes to client attraction, aka finding and engaging an audience.

By "rogue", I mean heading off and doing client attraction activities that I haven't approved. Because my job, part of what you pay me for, is to make that mess myself, figure it all out and then serve up refined and perfected strategies and assets that I've proven to be the most efficient and effective.

Success leaves clues, and the most successful tribe members, the ones generating six-figure results within the first 12 months, are using their precious minutes to learn and implement only the strategies that I give them so that they have the time for all the other things required to run a successful bookkeeping practice, and believe you me - there are many things - and so you can't afford to waste one moment on strategies that don't get you enough bang for buck.

Your time is finite; it's precious. Even if you can't see that right now, trust me now, and believe me later, every minute of your day will become your most precious resource. What I show you in this book and inside my program is designed to help you spend every minute on the highest value activities that will give you the biggest return on your time and money investment.

Existing audience

The "Existing Audience" strategy is exactly how I found my first client when I opened the doors to my bookkeeping practice way back in 2010. In my experience, this is how most bookkeepers find their first client, but they never stop to think about it as a strategy. But it is, my friend.

As I said a moment ago, it's critically important for you to be able to dissect your success.

If you are a bookkeeper in practice, take a moment right now to reflect on how you found your first client, then your second, and your third. Take a moment to dissect your success.

Was it someone you already knew? A friend of a friend? Someone referred to you? All of these roads lead back to one of the three strategies I've outlined here: existing audience, networking and EAPs.

As I outlined in my first book, your existing audience is all the people you're connected to in some way. These people are usually inside your social media, your phone, your email list, and your accounting software, and they include people you know through your hobbies and interests—like sports, church and school. I like to call your existing audience the "people I know network" and believe me, that network is probably much bigger than you can fathom right now. *An inch wide but a mile deep.*

These three strategies work like an ecosystem, feeding into one another. Let me give you an example.

Lessons from the tribe

Sandra joined our program in 2024, fairly new to owning and operating her own bookkeeping practice. Sandra's husband is an entrepreneur who runs a successful website development agency. Sandra decided to ask her husband if he would share one of her high-value **Welcome Line nurture assets** with his database as a gift to support them to do better in business, which he agreed to.

Sandra provided her husband with the free business fundamentals training she accessed in our program, along with our Better in Business Toolkit to complement it. This is easy for Sandra as it's all provided, done for her, in the Transformation Program. It's literally plug-and-play.

Sandra's husband, Steve, pressed go and sent this to his database (using the copy we gave Sandra), which resulted in some of Steve's audience becoming part of Sandra's audience as they filled in the form to register to get the business fundamentals training and the Better in Business Toolkit.

This is an example of how using your existing audience can connect you to an EAP. It shows how these three strategies tend to feed into one another.

Examples of existing audience activities you can do right now.

I mean, put down this book and do them! *Note: this will be a little rinse and repeat from my first book.*

Past and Inactive Clients

Reach out to your past and inactive clients by text message to say hi. Genuinely and authentically check in on them. For more on this, refer to the attraction chapter of my first book.

Personal Social Media

Jump onto your personal social media and tell all your business buddies you're open to business. Progress over perfection. If you join my program, we will give you a lot of support and assets on this, but right now, there's nothing wrong with a genuine, authentic post letting your friends know you are open for business.

I recently recommended to one of my tribe members, who is just starting out and ready to win her first client, that she make time in her diary once a week to do a post on her personal social media, calling attention to her entrepreneur friends and sharing one high-value welcome line nurture asset as a gift each week for 10 weeks.

Remember the pillar of persuasion reciprocity? Your welcome lines make great gifts for your entrepreneur friends because they're built to provide value to help them do better in business.

For entrepreneurs, social media has become a big digital networking room.

For more on this, refer to my first book.

Networking.

Remember I talked about getting bang for buck when it comes to marketing, of which finding and engaging an audience is a key component?

Well, when it comes to networking, some forms of networking work, and some don't.

When I say something doesn't work, I'm talking about return on investment. If you put enough time and energy into just about any strategy, eventually, you will get some results, even if they are very small.

Wasting your time on activities that give you a very small result is not how you build a thriving practice - it's how you build busy.

Structured networking works

My favourite form of structured networking is BNI, which stands for Business Networking International. As I demonstrated in my first book, I generated about a hundred thousand dollars in client work in my first year at Business Networking International.

In my first book, I give you a lot of information on how to make business networking work and actually, inside my starter membership, you'll find a workshop as well.

And because, unfortunately, most bookkeepers fail to make Networking work, even a world-class system like BNI, inside my program, the networking module is one of the most detailed. In addition to giving my tribe step-by-step instructions and a folder to create that contains their signature brochure and a checklist, I host coaching and implementation sessions regularly (on this subject), which are recorded and made available as videos and private podcasts.

To make networking work best and generate six figures in a year, you can't miss a beat. It's one of those strategies where you really do have to follow the system precisely. Where the devil really is in the detail.

It's also why, when it comes to business networking, in my program, I've provided all the marketing copy for bookkeepers to use, including their 45-second infomercial and so on. I also give bookkeepers the structure and strategy to deliver a presentation that hits the mark rather than missing the mark.

I can honestly say that if bookkeepers use my networking system to the letter, it works. And just as exciting is the fact that once it's working, they love business networking even though traditionally, bookkeepers tell me they hate business networking. When it works, when they are successful, and when the whole room is enjoying them, of course, I love it too, and it's so exciting to me.

Other forms of structured business networking

I advocate for any form of structured networking similar to BNI; however, in my experience, nothing works quite as well as BNI.

Casual networking doesn't work

I learnt from Ivan Misner, the founder of BNI, who's also known as the grandfather of networking and who you can listen to on my podcast, that at casual networking events,

100% of attendees go to sell and 0% go to buy, which I have found to be correct.

These days, networking happens in real life and online. An example of an online business networking group is Facebook groups like Women in Business or Business-Connect and so on; there are thousands.

What I am telling you here applies to both. Turning up in real life or online to casual networking groups, handing out your card and telling people **what** you do will get you nowhere, so don't do it; it's a waste of time, money, and energy.

Note: I have noticed that getting involved in your local community's Facebook page and networking inside of there can work. In my program, we have created some assets for our tribe to use in these community groups, which I call postcode groups. The members of these groups tend to have a common *purpose,* which is to support local businesses like yours, and so this is an activity I approve of.

We're always networking.

It's important to learn that in our business, we are always networking. And a key way to improve the results you get from networking with people around you is to improve your ability around The Six Pillars of Persuasion and to talk about the why – the benefits and outcomes – more than the how – which is what you'll do. As I said before, talk about the destination rather than the long-haul flight.

For example, let's say there's a tradie who's finished his job and is leaving the house. I'd give him my business card, and yes, I would mention that I am a bookkeeper. But because that's just talking about the long-haul flight, I'd also connect to my profile and results. I'd tell them I was recently Australian Bookkeeper of the Year, that I am currently the Women in Finance Australia Innovator of the Year and, most importantly, that I currently help tradies corner their market. By now, the tradie would be interested, and then I'd tell them how I recently took a business like theirs from bankruptcy to six figures in six months.

Now, you might be saying, well, Jeannie, I don't have those awards, and I haven't gotten those kinds of results with my clients. And my response is to say that together, we can build your profile and dive into the kind of results that you do have, which I'm sure can be made more impressive than you realise right now.

How it can work for you.

Inside my Program, my tribe become certified strategic bookkeepers to give them profile and a killer competitive advantage. They proudly display this badge in their collateral and talk about it in all the networking they do online and in real life. For example, their profile might say:

I am a certified strategic bookkeeper. We help entrepreneurs do better in business. Bookkeeping is a cost, whereas strategic bookkeeping is an investment that has helped hundreds of entrepreneurs optimise their profits, cash and time wealth.

We'll move on in a minute, but for now, what have you learnt about networking from my last book and this book? Can you see where networking has let you down in the past because you didn't quite know how to work it? What actions are you going to take to improve your networking performance?

Need to know more? Remember that I have lots more content for you on networking inside my podcast and starter membership and inside my program.

Evergreen Advocacy Partnerships (EAP).

An Evergreen Advocacy Partnership (EAP) is a mutual agreement whereby you and the partner agree to keep an eye out for opportunities to promote each other.

One way I've been explaining EAPs since publishing my last book is to liken finding an EAP to finding the shepherd of your ideal sheep. Or, as Daniel Priestly (another one of my mentors) puts it - stop looking for one client at a time and find a bunch of them - that's the power of EAP.

EAPs follow on nicely from networking because we often find them while networking. In fact, your goal when networking is not necessarily to find clients but to find partners who can help you while you help them.

Now, remember I told you that casual networking doesn't work. The exception is using casual networking to find an EAP. Let me explain

In the first five years of running my bookkeeping practice, I started to go to casual networking events, not to find clients, honestly, just for some adult company. As you probably know by now, I was going through a bit of a rough time dealing with the demands of a special needs child and a marriage that was going south. Networking with my peers at evening events, cocktail in hand, was a pretty lovely reprieve. As a side benefit, and maybe because I wasn't looking for clients, I struck up really lovely conversations and connected human-to-human with usually one or two people. From those connections, I was able to form partnerships.

Way back then, I didn't understand the details, the nuances, and the real strategy that would turbocharge these partnerships the way I understand it today. But the moral of that story is that casual networking can be super fun, and if you're going with the intention of making real connections with real people, it's a great way to find EAPs.

Just don't go with the intention of giving out your business card and telling everybody what you do - that will repel more people than it will attract. Go with the intention of relaxing and enjoying yourself, being yourself and making real connections.

When it comes to online casual networking, the only thing I approve of is reaching out to the group's founder/admin to set up a meeting to discuss whether there is a synergy that would benefit both of you and perhaps lead to forming a partnership—an EAP.

My top tips for making the EAP strategy work for you are

1. Work on developing a dozen EAP relationships
2. Of which you will end up with a top three that'll give you the biggest result in terms of growing your bookkeeping practice
3. I recommend you create a business development spreadsheet and reserve time each morning to contact potential EAPs
4. And also to set up activities with your existing EAPs
5. Remembering that the activity is to share a welcome line nurture asset with their database to build your database (and vice versa) - that means building your audience and nurturing your audience through the power of EAPs

Our tribe is going for big, impactful EAPs. I'll keep the supplier names top secret, but I will tell you that these are national companies serving thousands of their ideal clients who are thrilled to give our better-in-business tool kit to their business customers as a gift.

Paid & Summits

When I refer to paid, I am primarily referring to meta ads, aka Facebook and Instagram ads. Not so long ago, paid referred to Google AdWords.

Earlier, I mentioned Claire Pelletreau, one of my mentors. Claire is somewhat of a Guru when it comes to meta ads. Claire knows, and she teaches us that it is very hard to make meta-ads work to give you a return greater than your spend.

There are many moving parts to making meta ads and Summits work, and as Claire says, paid advertising will show you what's broken inside your business more often than generate sales.

Some of those moving parts are everything you see on the bookkeeping practice BluePrint. So you're going to have to learn and implement all these things and prove them in your business results before you can make paid advertising or Summits work for you - that would be Claire's advice, and that is my advice.

The economic tech and consumer landscape is changing every day. The front-end brand marketing and selling area of your business needs to keep pace with this change. Lucky for you, this is my zone of genius, and I absolutely love this stuff and so I'm continually educating myself to stay up to date to help you.

As I mentioned earlier, as a rule, the age-old principles of brand, marketing and selling don't change, but the application changes constantly. Again, this is in stark contrast to the backend administration of your practice, which is quite black and white and linear and much easier to get right.

This is why most coaches and programs miss the mark here, on the front-end stuff. This is also why The Strategic Bookkeeper has become known as a world-class world first in providing the team, education, assets, implementation and support around brand, marketing and selling that translates into 6 figure life-changing results.

Lessons From The Tribe on paid advertising

One of our very successful tribe members, Laura, had worked with a well-known bookkeeping coach who focuses on paid advertising. Laura spent over $50,000 and could not get a return greater than what she had spent. Inside the transformation program, Laura was able to get fully booked with a waitlist of high-value clients without paid advertising.

At the strategic bookkeeper, we are planning a summit to benefit our tribe through our better-in-business platform. This puts our tribe in front of an audience of entrepreneurs globally and sell the benefits of strategic bookkeeping over traditional bookkeeping - a kind of done-for-you lead generation.

That said, I am happy for bookkeepers like Laura, who've learned and implemented everything inside the transformation program, to consider running a Summit once they're educated and ready (and if they have the desire to do so). And we'll be there to guide and help her.

Engaging your audience.

While exploring how to find an audience, we have naturally explored how to nurture that audience using your product ladder—

specifically, your content and your welcome line nurture assets.

And I hope that this is all sounding quite logical. To generate enquiries from prospective clients, you need to

1. Find an audience, or as Claire Pelletreau says, find eyeballs
2. Nurture that audience onto your database
3. And then continue to nurture that audience to become a pipeline

To rinse and repeat from my first book, the essence of nurturing your database is KIT marketing, which stands for "keep in touch". You need to keep in touch with your database strategically, not spamming them, not telling them about the long-haul flight, but rather, giving them value.

Our Better in Business podcast is a great example of how to keep in touch with your beautiful humans in a way that serves to help them do better in business - that's value, and that's KISS - keeping it super simple.

To illustrate more about nurturing your audience, I'll turn to the tribe.

Lessons From The Tribe

There are many stories about audience engagement I could share with you, but here's one from a Business Development Challenge I ran in 2024 as part of my Program.

To give that some context, I'd opened the doors to the Program about nine months earlier, and while my tribe was growing, I was learning more from the tribe every day.

I'd already realised that a missing piece of the puzzle for most bookkeepers is business development. So, I created an entire module around that. Actually, the BluePrint you're using now was born that day - partly because I wanted to connect how business development worked with everything else – how it was different to other marketing activities, how to do it, and why it was important.

So, I was inducting a group of new members into the program, and I ended up asking, would you like me to run a business development challenge? The answer was a loud yes.

So we started the challenge, where I went live daily for three weeks of coaching. At the same time, my right hand, Jo McMahon, ran a price rise challenge so that everybody could do their annual price rise together. Both of these challenges were incredibly successful, and of course, we recorded them, so they're still included in the transformation program, and I refer to them regularly.

One of the participants was a tribe member named Angela – someone I'd describe as a quiet achiever. She doesn't say much (she's more of an observer), but she listens and then decisively takes action step by step. I'm pretty sure Angela turned up to pretty much every session over three weeks, engaging and asking some questions and making her notes. It was a great group in the challenge – a variety of passionate achievers and quiet achievers, with some tribe members pushing back and challenging me on the activities I asked them to do. Which, I must say, is perfect. Speaking up and speaking your mind is encouraged inside the program.

So there's Angela, not saying a lot but definitely participating, and as we progressed in the challenge, the various tribe members took action, and it was great to hear from them about the results they were getting.

One tribe member used our 20-minute call process to reach out to an existing client to begin the process that ultimately upgrades them from basic to strategic bookkeeping. To do that we use our product ladder; specifically, the process includes a business health check and now/future analysis, along with on-point, done-for-you marketing copy that goes in an email. It invites the client to do the diagnostic themselves and book straight into your calendar to review their results.

This bookkeeper was always reluctant to do this activity, as she was someone who wanted to focus primarily on finding new business, but she trusted me, and she did it. She told me the client said he'd never had service like that. He was dazzled and delighted, and sure enough, he upgraded.

Anyway, back to Angela. She's so quiet; she just gets on with it. But she diligently applied herself to the business development activities around existing audiences and networking and EAPs that I asked everyone to do in the challenge, as well as taking care of all the elements of the BluePrint. Making sure they dialed in all the parts of the BluePrint and using me for support to do so was part of the challenge. And honestly, it's easy inside the program because of the done-for-you elements.

So, bearing in mind that Angela was pretty new to the program (just a few months in) she built out her audience just as I showed her. She engaged that audience with the welcome line nurture assets we gave her, and within a few months, she told me quietly she was booked solid and actually now over capacity.

Shortly after, Angela asked if she could graduate the program early and step into our graduate program. Now, the transformation program is self-paced, and while it is rare to see bookkeepers graduate early, absolutely they can. So Angela levelled up from becoming a certified Strategic Bookkeeper to becoming a world-class entrepreneur, which is what is waiting for our tribe at the end of their first lap around the sun – the Graduate Club.

How Angie did it.

- Nailing the left-hand side of the BluePrint was easy for Angie to do inside the program. As I've already mentioned, most of it's done for you.

- In terms of finding an audience, Angie leaned into existing audience and EAPs primarily to build her database.
- Angie's audience had a great brandsphere to float around in - her website and social media - with all the strategies and assets developed by our team.
- As we license our tribe to set up a private Facebook group called "better in business with..." Angie did that, too - using the brand assets we gave her
- Existing Audience - Entire database - Angie nurtured her entire database by sending them the Better in Business podcast fortnightly - this is plug and play; the email is done for you and updated in the academy fortnightly.
- Existing Audience - clients - she also nurtured her clients with our 20-minute call process, which seeks to connect on a deeper level, which naturally leads to upgrades from basic bookkeeping to strategic bookkeeping (advisory and so on) - this is a "diagnostics pack"
- EAPs: Angie gave her EAPs a Business Fundamentals Training to provide their database and then nurtured the audience that came through registrations (in the same way she nurtures everyone)

- Angie also posted her on-demand Business Fundamentals Training - recorded webinar - on social media platforms, which generated more audience to nurture
- Angie did other "Marketing Layering" activities that we teach inside the program, like winning awards and getting more reviews.
- She used all the welcome line nurture assets in her kit at appropriate times to nurture her audience with massive value.
- Looking at the BluePrint, you will see that Angie was nurturing her database passively – the audience she was finding from any of her activities was dropping into her database, ready to be engaged and nurtured.
- Critically, Angie spent time on business development activities every single morning – following up with clients that she'd invited to take part in the 20-minute call, seeking out new EAPs and cultivating her existing advocacy partners, following up on client proposals, and so on. We strongly recommend time every morning for business development activities, and for Angie it worked beautifully.

So you'll see that there's a fair bit about nurturing your database in that example, so I think it's appropriate to delve into that topic a bit more deeply. Before you do, just ask yourself, what content do you currently have in your product ladder to engage your market with?

Nurturing your database.

I don't really need to go into too much detail here because I've covered this subject so comprehensively in The Strategic Bookkeeper (it's all part of Chapter 4 - The Power of Attraction).

But to rinse and repeat, which is good for the memory, let's do a quick recap.

Look at your network's network.

For every name on your database, there's an entire network of people that you may be able to tap into - an inch wide, a mile deep. Every client has an accountant, a lawyer, an insurance broker, a real estate agent – the list just goes on and on. So what you want to do is enrol your database's database. Get them to float into your brandsphere and do a little farming.

It starts with messaging.

If there was only one marketing professional I could hire, it'd be a copywriter. Strategic messaging is a key element in nurturing your audience and conveying the benefits of hiring a Strategic Bookkeeper. Or, as we like to say, "Fire your bookkeeper and hire a Strategic Bookkeeper" - now that's great copy!

That's why we have several marketing copywriters at team HQ to provide our tribe with this all done-for-them. Hiring a copywriter to do even the basics would cost you well in excess of the program fee and is another example of a cost you won't incur if you are in the tribe.

Choose your platforms.

While a lot of your communications with your database will be via email, it's important to replicate it on social media, too. This gives people who are floating in and out of your brandsphere a chance to see and be persuaded by your strategic marketing copy - your messaging.

But be consistent! If you're not going to post regularly (3 times a week), shut your social media down until you can do that - otherwise, it'll damage your credibility because you'll appear either closed, failing or disorganised.

More on this in my first book.

In the program, we give you a social media strategy plus a regularly updated library of social media posts to use. Just yesterday I went live in our private members Facebook group to provide some direction on social media and mention that team HQ are diving deep into AI because this will impact it.

I've said it before, and I'll say it again; the application of brand, marketing and selling changes with the moving economic, tech and consumer landscape - you have to keep up. My tribe pays me to keep up and then simply update them - that's what our 6-figure team does.

Tribe members sometimes ask me, "Jeannie, if I'm a solo operator, should I use "I" rather than "we" in my collateral?" I remind them that the day you join TSB, you have a team—you're a "we." You have a marketing department, and so on. Plus, before you know it, you'll likely be using our recruitment BluePrint to onboard a full-time allrounder.

If you're with us inside the program, you only need to dedicate an hour to social media per month. And once your full time all-rounder is onboard, they'll do that along with all the other admin.

Remember the customer journey.

Selling is dead; self-assessing is in. This is also known as the death of marketing and the rise of PR.

One of the first things we teach you in the Transformation Program is the customer journey—you can read more about that in the attraction chapter of my first book.

To rinse and repeat a little, your audience needs to go through the customer journey, spend time in your brandsphere, get to know, like and trust you 24/7 online, being influenced by the six pillars of persuasion - exactly the same way you do when looking for products and services.

Going through your smart, strategic customer journey, which includes your product ladder and your on-point marketing copy, they'll self-assess into Strategic Bookkeeping, which is how a pipeline is built.

Key Learnings from this chapter

Now it's time to review the 10-point plan I gave you at the beginning of this chapter, and I'd love to know if it all makes more sense now.

What have you learned?

What will you do?

Whether it makes a little sense or a lot of sense, your success will begin with mindset mastery, my friend. I'll continue to elaborate on this because every day, I see more and more evidence that what holds us back is not the mechanics (the stuff we need to do); it's our mindset first and a lack of productivity second.

So, right now, you might be at another fork in the road. In one direction, negative self-talk like, "I can't do this"; in the other, self-talk like, "I can do this" along with a commitment to just keep going... Some of the most successful people on this planet got there because they just kept going. Keep this top secret, but I'm one of them, and so is my father.

I really do hope you just keep going, like Edison did when he was trying to invent the light bulb.

On that front, would you do something for me? Would you take a moment right now to take a breath, reset, and simply say something positive to yourself, like... "I am receiving all good things?"

Ok, back to the mechanics.

Your 10-point plan is how you find and engage an audience to become a pipeline. So, to build a thriving practice with delighted clients and your dream on your terms:

1. Focus on the first three audience-building strategies.
2. Remember to nail the BluePrint with proven results before trying the last two.
3. Every one of the audience-building strategies is an inch wide and a mile deep - you can work these forever, and they will build you a 6 or 7-figure thriving practice when combined with nailing the BluePrint.
4. Therefore, on these three strategies, keep asking yourself... what else, what else, what else?
5. Create a business development spreadsheet to use to work on these strategies.

6. Put your database in there so you can categorise and see them visually - that way, you'll connect with your database more deeply, human to human and be more likely to keep in touch with them in a relevant, authentic way.
7. Do also use a CRM like Mailchimp or https://www.officiently.com.au/ to do your strategic keep-in-touch marketing.
8. Reserve time each morning to work on activities related to building and engaging your audience - new and existing.
9. Once you find an audience, get them onto your database and then nurture them with your product ladder.
10. Do both passive and active activities - active being putting on the business development hat.

Let's move on.

In the chapter you've just finished, we did a bit of rinsing and repeating from the attraction chapter of my first book. Client attraction is listed as bookkeeper bugbear #2 after number #1, which is getting paperwork from clients. It's also what 68% of entrepreneurs say is their toughest challenge, and so I think it begs repeating, don't you?

Now, let's put on our business development hats and tackle the last big chapter and the last major aspect of the BluePrint related to brand, marketing and selling.

Chapter 7 - Wearing Your Business Development Hat

We are on the home stretch, my friend. You've now got a handle on all the moving parts of the BluePrint from what I've shared in this book, along with what I shared in my first book.

As I sit here writing, I'm imagining you reading or listening to this book. I'm picturing that your head might be spinning a little bit. Thinking back to the beginning of my journey, if I'd gotten my hands on a book like this, I would have been mind-blown.

Discovering the bookkeeping practice BluePrint, discovering what's required to build a successful bookkeeping practice—one with high profits, happy clients, and scaled to a point where it really is a business (rather than a job), with a team and tech, and the rewards of the income and time that, let's face it, you started it for— discovering this could be a bit overwhelming.

I want to address that feeling of overwhelm for a moment. Right now, as I sit here writing, it's just after 9:00 a.m. on a Thursday, and in a few minutes, I'm going to jump into an impromptu hot seat with one of our new tribe members. I've posted the Zoom link in our private community so everyone can take advantage of some open coaching on anything and everything. You see, today is the first day of our newest cohort's first lap around the sun in the transformation program. I'm so excited, and they are too.

Just half an hour ago, I jumped into our private Facebook group and did a live video welcoming everyone in, but I also shared some important stuff to help everyone succeed.

One of the things I shared was a couple of rules we have here at The Strategic Bookkeeper HQ. The first one is that - *we never say, "I know."* I reminded everyone that saying this closes us off to personal and professional growth. This time, I added another phrase I want to ban from our language—including my own—and that is, *"I can't."*

In my first book, I shared with you something I learned from my father, that we can never exceed our own expectations of ourselves. If you or I say, *"I can't,"* I'm pretty sure you can't. But if you say, *"I can,"* I'm pretty confident you'll get there - certainly, if you're with me inside my program, I am 100% sure you can. 100%!

In conversations with bookkeepers, I've noticed that *"I can't"* is often followed by *"I know"* and then by *"I'm overwhelmed."* It's a bit of a domino series. When we use language like this, we set our expectations of ourselves very low. I'm pretty sure that if you say, *"I can't,"* *"I know,"* and *"I'm overwhelmed,"* then that will become your reality.

Our thoughts and our words create our reality. Choose them wisely. Set your expectations of yourself high rather than low.

Shoot for the moon.

Even if you miss, you'll land among the stars. This beautiful metaphor reminds you to aim for the highest achievements, even if they feel out of reach. By striving for greatness, even if you don't hit your exact goal, you'll still achieve something extraordinary. So, aim big.

In terms of learning and implementing everything in the BluePrint—yes, there's a lot, and yes, that's what it takes to be part of the 10% of bookkeepers making six figures rather than 90% making less than a decent job pays—I am here for you, and the program is here for you.

It puzzles me why bookkeepers struggle on even when they know the results their peers are getting inside our Transformation Program, but I live from a place of faith, not fear, and I've come to realise that fear is the root of what keeps us stuck in the safety of inaction.

I know this from experience, my friend.

Living from a place of faith didn't fall ass-first out of the sky for me. I worked for it, and I continue to - to this day. I work on my shame and my vulnerability. I embrace being *"a beautifully flawed human being stumbling along with the illusion of control ©"*.

In 2023, I let go of fear, followed my Dharma (purpose) and brought The Strategic Bookkeeper to the world. Supporting bookkeepers all over the globe now fills my cup.

It is now my privilege and my pleasure to support you on your journey as a bookkeeper in practice, to build the business and life of your dreams, and to positively impact the lives of those around you, which is a legacy you'll leave behind.

I could never have done this without letting go of fear.

If fear is holding you back from anything you covet in life, I hope that this book sparks a fire that might move you to the other side of that fear, to faith.

The brand, marketing and selling ecosystem

Before we dive into the what, the why and the how of business development, I want to review the parts of the bookkeeping practice BluePrint that we've gone over so far, specifically around brand, marketing and selling and how they all connect with the business development hat.

You've built your *brand*, your beautiful, ethereal organisation-personality that you'll showcase in your *brand assets* - a lot like how you show up in your Sunday best (dress). Your brand is ready to greet your *audience* and connect with them, making them want to hang out with you. Once you start making friends (pc's), you'll keep in touch with them passively via email and social media, courting them with gifts (welcome line nurture assets) that will help them do better in business, making them love you and spread the word about what a cool cat you are (advocacy in your market).

Of course, the more audience your brand gets in front of, the more friends you'll make - who you can nurture with your gifts, right?

Business success is somewhat of a maths equation like that - a numbers game.

Now, through the power of human psychology, the fact our brains don't distinguish between digital and real, the audience that you are nurturing will be getting to know, like and trust you 24/7 online just as if they were at the dinner table with you, which is really cool - it's way more scalable than trying to do everything in person.

If you create a big enough audience and you nurture them, this will create a bit of a lineup at your door, a pipeline of people who want to meet you in real life and get your help to solve their problems.

Thanks to the power of tech, team, automation, AI and robotics - a lot of this can be built and then put on auto-pilot, which is awesome, and, once again, scalable.

There's just one more high-value activity you need to be/do/have to complete this beautiful brand, marketing and selling ecosystem, and that's... business development.

What is business development?

It's typical for organisations, especially larger, departmentalised ones, to hire business development managers. And broadly, a business development manager, is a salesperson. It's a sales role.

You know, you've seen them, you probably know one.

They will have many tasks and duties, and these can range from business networking to following up on quotes. The objective is always the same - to generate more business, which is to generate Sales - sales that may come from existing clients or new clients, sales that may come directly or indirectly through partners and so on. You get the gist.

The nature of the Bookkeeping practice model requires the owner to be the business development manager.

While everything has the meaning we give it, I want to define business development for you as a bookkeeper in practice - that's my job - to laser-focus everything for bookkeepers.

In terms of finding and engaging an audience, let's discuss passive vs. active.

When you attend a networking event, that is an example of a business development activity. You're actively getting out there, connecting with people. When your networking group joins your database, and you begin to send them your better-in-business podcast fortnightly (if you're in my tribe, for example), that's an example of a more passive marketing activity.

Both are important, and both are required. Here are a dozen key business development activities that you could and should be doing regularly.

1. Attend your regular networking event
2. Do your dance cards (catch-ups) with networking buddies
3. Reach out to a potential EAP
4. Have a meeting with an existing EAP
5. Do an EAP activity like - sending a nurture asset to their database

6. Send a text message to a hot, "proposal out" prospect
7. Send a text message to a prospect who went elsewhere or went cold
8. Send a text message to a past client, checking in
9. Send a text message to an inactive client, checking in
10. Send a text message to a client to follow up on booking the 20-minute call process
11. Telephone a client to do your monthly check-in
12. Send a text message to registrants of an on-demand (or live) event, training or webinar you have on autopilot.

Why you need to do business development activities

To dive into this I'll start with a quote from Matt Wilkinson, the founder of Bizink, the world's best web developer for bookkeepers and accountants - "A website won't bring you clients - business development will bring you clients".

To be clear, your website is a critically important brand asset that forms part of your brand, marketing and selling ecosystem. As is finding and engaging your audience.

Business development is the piece of the puzzle that turbo charges the "win the work" side of business. Here's an example...

Lessons from the Tribe

Do you remember Kelly's story that I shared with you earlier? The story about scarcity? This is a perfect example of business development in action and the results you can expect.

Kelly's prospect, Tom, had been sitting on his proposal for a month before one text message, incorporating the scarcity pillar of persuasion, made Tom press go.

If you skip the business development activities you'll miss out on sales, that's for sure. Whereas if you just go that little bit further and do these "active things", your pipeline will fill up even more, you'll grow and scale faster.

In my first book, I share more examples of results generated from business development activities.

How to wear the business development hat

With a rock-solid structure and process, that's how.

Before we dive into this, I feel I need to mention the busy bookkeeper again. I regularly get emails from busy bookkeepers who tell me, *"I want to join your program, but I just don't have the time."*

This breaks my heart because it's a cycle that they'll usually stay stuck in forever, believing the time will magically appear, often believing that more revenue will create more time, unaware they're working with a broken business model building busy, not thriving.

When bookkeepers join my tribe they tell me - *"that's me Jeannie, I'm busy but I want to be thriving"* and together step by step we get there.

If you join my program, the team and I will work our bums off to help you master your mindset, become highly productive, and get it done.

Let's move on.

Here's what I recommend you do, in a structured way, to wear the business development hat, increase your pipeline, win more work, grow and scale:

BLUEPRINT

1. Create a business development spreadsheet as a workbook
2. List the one dozen business development activities I've given you on a worksheet within your workbook, which you can use as your primary dashboard.
3. Populate another worksheet with your entire email database (and do a little categorisation) so you can see your humans visually, which will encourage you to actually reach out to them actively - to connect with them.
4. Reserve time each morning before you work "in your business" to do business development activities (that's working on your business)
5. The more activities you do, the more business you'll generate in your practice (yup, it's like a sales lever you can pull)
6. If you want to do all 12 daily, fantastic. If you only do one a day, fantastic - it's probably one more than you've been doing, and it will move the needle if you play the long game and be patient.

The key is to approach this in a process-driven, methodical and repetitive way.

One reason this approach is important is that, as a rule, bookkeepers aren't built to be business development managers, and that's okay—the system will get you there.

In my program, I use systems (and assets) to turn bookkeepers like you into world-class sales professionals, converting 90% of PCs into high-value, raving fan clients. Systems rock. Lean into systems.

One of the mistakes I see some bookkeepers make around financial management is deciding to recruit someone to do these type of marketing and selling activities. Their logic is "I'm not good at this, I can't do this, I'll just pay someone else to do it". Trust me now, and believe me later, it's not financially viable, and it rarely works out.

Once your practice is booked solid and on the waitlist, you can do less active and more passive if you want. That's what I did in my practice and that's what a lot of my tribe do.

Pull the business development lever when you need to.

Also, bear in mind that once you scale into "booked-solid" with a waitlist, it makes sense to focus your energy on succession which is solving more problems for your VIP clients with high value, high impact advisory like "Strategic Bookkeeping".

Lessons from the tribe

Here is a great lesson about scaling your bookkeeping practice and then choosing how much business development you do or don't do.

Tracy joined my programme in 2023, not long after we opened the doors to our programme. This post is from October 2024, with results achieved within 12 months.

Tracy

I did the program for one year. It will help you change your pricing structure and, therefore, increase revenue. It will also assist you in marketing and networking and show you how to engage a team. I also think a little manifestation is at play.

I managed to replace the income I received from a high-paying job and now work a few hours per week, checking the work of my team.

I fired a few clients and picked up new ones along the way and Jeannie shows you how to value what you do and helps change your beliefs. The tribe are very supportive too.

This is a great work-life balance for me. My (second) husband is retired, and I couldn't afford to retire with him, but now I work part-time and earn well over $100k pa.

Yes, I could build up the business more, but I'm loving where I'm at right now.

I don't believe you'll regret it if you follow the process.

To give context to Tracy's post, it was in response to this question in "The Strategic Bookkeeper's Way" Facebook group, which is free to join...

Hello! I'm not sure if posting is okay, but I was hoping to get some more info on the strategic bookkeeping program.

I am trying to grow my bookkeeping practice so I can have a better work-life balance that fits with me and the limitations my disability gives me.

I would love some advice or support to understand the program a bit better.

I am very desperate to grow my business and so unsure how to do that.

Thanks for your time!

My intention when educating you around how to wear the business development hat is to KISS - keep it super simple.

You learn by doing, so get out there and use everything I've taught you, including the checklists I've given you here.

Standard operating procedures

Standard operating procedures is the last item on the BluePrint. On this subject, I've already shared a treasure trove of information in my first book, in two chapters - Systems and Team.

I'd also like to point you to two podcasts on standard operating procedures which are episodes 71 and 81.

In episode 71, Claire Beckett will explain why and how she spent time rounding out her standard operating procedures for her team to use.

In episode 81, you're here from Karen Andrews, one of our tribe members who was already very successful, with a team of 10, when they joined us, and her journey around standard operating procedures.

If you look at the BluePrint, next to standard operating procedures, you'll see these two sub-headlines

- Promises kept
- Communication

This is what I'd like to dive a little deeper into in this book.

To begin with, I'll tell you what I told my tribe in open coaching this week.

Promises kept is the beating heart of your bookkeeping practice, and communication is the veins that the blood runs through.

Sound pretty important? Yup!

Getting this right is game-changing, and getting this wrong is devastating.

To explain this further, I'd like to share something with you that I shared with a brand-new tribe member recently in an impromptu Hot Seat.

Seed to flower
When you get a new client, you need to treat them like a seed: you want to water, feed and love them so that they grow into a flowering plant. To do that, you should spend the first few months getting to know them, getting to know all about them.

One of the key things you want to find out is the best way to communicate with them. If they're a tradie, like so many are, you will probably find they hate reading emails and would prefer a quick phone call. But you might find some prefer email; some might say, "I just want one email a month". Great.

In my practice, we use communication as a secret marketing weapon, and it helps us create happy raving fan clients who stay with us irrespective of price and refer others to us.

One of our core values is empathy, and we aim to treat our clients how they want to be treated, not how we want to be treated. Yup, that's right - *do not treat others as you wish to be treated; treat them as they want to be treated.*

Communication is a key area that I see 100% of bookkeepers can improve in to improve client satisfaction, retention, and profitability.

As I said in my first book, "there is nothing more important than keeping your promise to your clients as well as your prospective clients—that's trust and that's integrity." I've talked about this extensively in my first book, so I'll let you go back and rinse and repeat.

Gratitude and Self Love

We're at the end of this book, my friend, but hopefully not the end of our journey together.

When I launched The Strategic Bookkeeper Project, I told my team, "I'll go to the grave having changed our industry for the better." So, how am I doing?

I'd love to hear from you, and you can connect with me here www.facebook.com/groups/thestrategicbookkeepersway

I want to take this opportunity to express my deep gratitude to bookkeepers from all over the world who've reached out, shared their thoughts, and let me know how my work has impacted them. Messages like the one I received from a woman in Tanzania, East Africa, seeking support to do better in business and life... they fill my cup.

Helping women across the globe step out from the shadows of insecurity and into the confidence of knowing their worth is what gets me up each morning and keeps me inspired all day.

We've talked a lot about mindset in this book, and I have one final request *of you*. It's about self-celebration—something I also teach my son.

At the time of writing this, my son is 14, navigating puberty, and he's neurodiverse. I've seen him struggle with negative self-talk, and as a mum, it's heartbreaking. So, I've been encouraging him to love and celebrate himself as much as he does others, to treat himself as kindly as he treats the people he loves and cares about. This is something we rarely do for ourselves.

I often ask him, "Who loves ya, kid?" and he usually replies, "You do, Mum." Recently, though, he answered, "I do, Mum. I love myself." I was so thrilled.

So, I'm asking you to do the same: to spend just one day (maybe one day that becomes many) truly celebrating yourself. What would that look like? What would you say or do differently?

When I launched "The Strategic Bookkeeper", I was immensely proud of what I'd created. While building my new office, I thought, "Why not celebrate with a neon sign that reads "Jeannie Savage" to hang prominently in the space?" When I shared this idea with a friend, she said, "Oh no, you can't do that. Just get a small sign and put it in the corner," as if I should minimise myself. At first, I was triggered, and for a moment, I bought into it. But then I thought, "No". I chose to celebrate myself—which isn't always the easiest thing to do, but this form of self-love is so important.

So, whether it's a neon sign or something else, do what makes you feel celebrated. Don't apologise for positive self-talk or for loving and honouring yourself just as you do others.

You're ready to fly.

I'm a multi-tasking Mum who started a bookkeeping practice and quickly realised that working all hours on the books while scrambling around trying to get new clients was no way to earn the financial and time freedom I know I deserve.

So, through years of trial, error, refinement, testing and application, I created the category and techniques of strategic bookkeeping. The masterpiece and cornerstone of my success is the BluePrint. Followed faithfully and diligently, it's a guaranteed recipe for success.

Now, I've harped on about this in every chapter – and you know that when I rinse and repeat anything, it's because I need you to take it seriously – but please, please use this book as it is intended, as a partner and valuable addition to my first book, *The Strategic Bookkeeper.*

And if you follow my instructions and read both books through twice – once for a general understanding and a second time for practice and internalisation – I promise you, you'll learn a hell of a lot about strategic bookkeeping, and the branding, marketing, sales and management practices that go along with it.

And as always, my tribe and I stand ready to welcome you into our ranks. Working with us, you'll fly through the processes of building a strategic bookkeeping practice and crafting your BluePrint assets, because we'll do so much of it for you and with you.

Whether you join us or not, I wish you the very best of success and freedom. The world needs more strategic bookkeepers, and I'm sure you'll bring credit to our profession, however you go about it.

Gifts for our readers from our business buddies

Ignition Solo Plan:

🔗 Unique partner link:

https://info.ignitionapp.com/bksoloplan-eoi?utm_source=partner_influencer&utm_content=-jeannie-savage&utm_campaign=10-APAC-Events-DGQ42024-solo-plan-launch-jeannie-savage

The Solo plan is designed specifically for solopreneurs and is restricted to one Ignition user

license and 20 active clients. To qualify for the Solo plan, your business must earn less than

$200,000 in annual revenue. Upon sign up, you'll also need to connect your Xero, MYOB or

QuickBooks Online accounting software to Ignition, and enable payments.

Plan details:

- $49/month ($39/month billed annually)
- 20 active clients (+7 per additional active client)
- 1 user account

Dext:

https://infl.tv/lJZl

1 month free of Dext prepare

You can Prepare, sort and automatically publish paperwork using Prepare with Receipt Bank.

- Pull cost data from over 1,400 suppliers and automatically sort and categorise with smart supplier rules.
- Match paperwork with cost data through bank connections for reconciliation.
- Use our smart tools to analyse tax, payment timing and talk to your clients about cashflow, all in real time.

(Please ask for the special rates for our Tribe which should be 20% off or, as at 19.11.23 $20 per file)

BizInk - Website Design

https://www.bizinkonline.com/

https://www.bizinkonline.com/book-a-demo/

You need to say you're part of TSB

They have website packages that are due to start from $50 per month, including hosting.

- Monthly website subscription @ $99 AUD
  - o For bookkeeper - 50% off first month
- Annual @ $990
  - o Get 12 months, pay for 10

Links

Chapter 1

Page 1 - The Strategic Bookkeeper E-book, *My secret sauce to creating a thriving practice by becoming a strategic bookkeeper*

https://www.thestrategicbookkeeper.global/book

Page 6 - Business Blueprint

https://www.thestrategicbookkeeper.global/blueprintresources

Page 8 - Starter Membership

https://www.thestrategicbookkeeper.global/starter

Page 9 - The Strategic Bookkeepers way Facebook Group

https://www.facebook.com/groups/thestrategicbookkeepersway

Chapter 2

Page 8 - Brain Model

https://www.thestrategicbookkeeper.global/blueprintresources

Page 20 - Priority List

https://www.thestrategicbookkeeper.global/tsb

Chapter 3

Page 2 - Business playbook

https://www.thestrategicbookkeeper.global/blueprintresources

Business Playbook Template.docx

Page 8 - The Strategic Bookkeeper E-book, *My secret sauce to creating a thriving practice by becoming a strategic bookkeeper*

https://www.thestrategicbookkeeper.global/book

Chapter 4

Page 1 - The Pricing Academy

https://www.thestrategicbookkeeper.global/pricingacademy

Page 2 - The Strategic Bookkeeper podcast Episode 88-TSB Success Panel

https://www.thestrategicbookkeeper.global/the-strategic-bookkeeper-podcast OR

https://spoti.fi/3CDoCL4 OR https://apple.co/3CCpmzX

Page 5 - Podcast 75 to 77 on 'Pricing for profit and joy

https://www.thestrategicbookkeeper.global/the-strategic-bookkeeper-podcast

Page 5 - Podcast Link for Episode 75-77 on 'pricing for profit and joy'

https://www.thestrategicbookkeeper.global/the-strategic-bookkeeper-podcast

EP75 : https://spoti.fi/3XC9Zzz OR https://apple.co/4fRy9gp

EP76 : https://spoti.fi/4d2mGZ8 OR https://apple.co/3AOYuwc

EP 77 : https://spoti.fi/3Zuuq2I OR https://apple.co/3V0XNqz

Episode 87

https://www.thestrategicbookkeeper.global/the-strategic-bookkeeper-podcast

https://spoti.fi/4fWforD OR https://apple.co/412vDiN

Episode 86

https://www.thestrategicbookkeeper.global/the-strategic-bookkeeper-podcast

https://spoti.fi/4i03pv2 OR https://apple.co/40VDL4i

Chapter 5

Page 6 - Better in Business podcast

https://www.betterinbusiness.global/podcast

Chapter 6

Page 2 - CRM system Offiently

https://www.officiently.com.au/

Chapter 7

Page 8 - Podcast Episode 71

https://www.thestrategicbookkeeper.global/the-strategic-bookkeeper-podcast

https://spoti.fi/3OhecTI OR https://apple.co/3AEu6ok

Page 8 - Podcast Episode 81

https://www.thestrategicbookkeeper.global/the-strategic-bookkeeper-podcast

https://spoti.fi/3ZknP9F OR https://apple.co/3V2hGgC

Page 10 - Facebook Link - The Strategic Bookkeepers Way

www.facebook.com/groups/thestrategicbookkeepersway

www.ingramcontent.com/pod-product-compliance
Lightning Source LLC
Chambersburg PA
CBHW042116190326
41519CB00030B/7517